The Three C's
Communication, Customer Service, & Chatbots

I. Edmondson

BookLocker

Trenton, Georgia

Print ISBN: 978-1-958891-09-4
Ebook ISBN: 979-8-88531-598-2

Published by BookLocker.com, Inc., Trenton, Georgia.

BookLocker.com, Inc.
2024

First Edition

Library of Congress Cataloguing in Publication Data
Edmondson, I.
The Three C's: Communication, Customer Service, & Chatbots by I. Edmondson
Library of Congress Control Number: 2023919009

DISCLAIMER

This book details the author's personal experiences with and opinions about the changes that according to various reports have and are occurring in communication, customer service, and the use of chatbots in various aspects of the world.

The author and publisher are providing this book and its contents on an "as is" basis and make no representations or warranties of any kind with respect to this book or its contents. The author and publisher disclaim all such representations and warranties, including for example warranties of merchantability and personal or business advice for a particular purpose. In addition, the author and publisher do not represent or warrant that the information accessible via this book is accurate, complete or current.

The statements made about products and services have not been evaluated by the U.S. government. Please consult with your own legal, accounting, medical, or other licensed professional regarding the suggestions and recommend-dations made in this book.

Except as specifically stated in this book, neither the author or publisher, nor any authors, contributors, or other representatives will be liable for damages arising out of or in connection with the use of this book. This is a comprehend-sive limitation of liability that applies to all damages of any kind, including (without limitation) compensatory; direct, indirect or consequential damages; loss of data, income or profit; loss of or damage to property and claims of third parties.

PREFACE

Customer service requires interaction, and its delivery is considered vital to every company's success. In the 1990's, the World Wide Web made it possible to continue the person-to-person customer service had always been provided but with added dimensions: e-mails, websites, help pages, helpdesks, and live chat. Customer Service is no longer dependent ONLY on direct human contact because in the 2000s, social media opened the door even wider.

Ongoing scientific advances make it possible to extend the ways in which direct relationships are made possible, and by 2010, remote maintenance and faster service were possible because of the use of tools such as TeamViewer. It showed companies that not only is the quality of their products or services important, but their products should also be backed by a strong support team and an effective approach. Currently, this necessitates a focus on the automation of communication channels and the introduction of new tools such as Chatbots. Things are changing rapidly, and now the question is, "What will education, customer service, business, and communication demands be 200 years from now?

A "thank you" goes to Kim and Michael Kearney for their support throughout the research of this book.

I.Edmondson

TABLE OF CONTENTS

CHAPTER 1: THE KEYS TO CUSTOMER SERVICE SUCCESS 1

CHAPTER 2: WHAT ROLE DOES "AI PLAY?..................13

CHAPTER 3: THE CUSTOMER ALWAYS COMES FIRST 25

CHAPTER 4: GIVE THEM WHAT THEY EXPECT, AND YOU'LL GET WHAT YOU WANT – SUCCESS! 41

CHAPTER 5: WHERE HAVE WE BEEN AND WHERE ARE WE GOING? 59

CHAPTER 6: LET'S MAKE IT PERSONAL 75

CHAPTER 7: THE ONLY THING CONSTANT IS CHANGE.. 111

CHAPTER 8: COULD MACHINES REPLACE HUMANS? 145

CHAPTER 9: WHAT ROLE CAN AI PLAY IN IMPROVING CUSTOMER SERVICE?.....................169

CHAPTER 10: DOING BUSINSS IN 2023......................191

CHAPTER 11: THE KEY STEPS TO DELIVERING MEMORABLE CUSTOMER SERVICE 219

CHAPTER 12: TEACHERS FACE NEW EDUCATIONAL CHALLENGES 251

CHAPTER 13: WHERE DID WE GO WRONG? 259

CHAPTER 14: WHERE DO WE GO FROM HERE?......281

I. Edmondson

CHAPTER 15: ARE WE PREPARED FOR
    WHAT'S TO COME?...309

BIBLIOGRAPHY 329

AFTERWARD...335

CHAPTER 1:
THE KEYS TO CUSTOMER SERVICE SUCCESS

HOW WINNERS USE ARTIFICIAL INTELLIGENCE

As it is for almost everything in today's society, artificial intelligence is now playing a part in customer service. Two-thirds of this generation expects—no, demands--real time customer service, and the cost for that service is rising at a rate never before known. For many companies, cost factors make the addition of already well-trained employees a non-option, so companies are now searching for alternative ways to meet that demand.

Many are now turning to "AI" to deliver the personalized service demanded because it can be used to increase the available service while reducing the cost of many aspects of that process. For example, a study conducted by McKinsey & Co. (a global management consulting firm) showed that in global banking, AI technologies were estimated to be able to deliver "up to one trillion dollars of additional services per year and thus revamped customer service accounts thereby providing a major portion of the services needed.

As amazing as it may sound to those who have been part of the generations used to having their customer service delivered mainly by humans, "AI" may well be able to deliver better personalized service than was ever possible before and do so faster than when only humans were handling the process. Now, that doesn't mean that the personal approach won't be missed, but the speed of the response will, for many, make up for that loss.

A number of areas will need to be revamped in order to make it possible to provide a better level of customer service. The routine questions such as delivery dates, balances owed, and order status are among the frequently posed questions that can now be answered by Chatbots (an artificial intelligence developed to interactively collect or provide information to customers) -- the data needed can then be stored in internal systems for later use. When that is done, the human support staff can handle the more complex questions, and operational costs can be reduced.

True, the overall service will be less personalized, but, for the most part, customers are not as interested in personalization if they are getting their problems solved and their questions answered quickly. One of the greatest annoyances for most customers is a "long wait" before the desired service is given or the question is handled.

Also, there are definite financial benefits as far as the involved companies are concerned. When automation is used to update records, provide a proactive outreach to customers, or handle minor questions or problems, it not only improves efficiency but can also reduce costs. In such cases. not only are the customer's needs met more quickly and efficiently, but the companies probably save millions of dollars yearly in time-related costs. None of that can happen, however, unless there is training. Computers are nothing without that training. "We need people thinking about what the computer is going to do," said Peter Blignaut, manager of pre-sales at SAP South Africa during a keynote address. "Machines don't learn from other machines; people must teach them."

AI can be used to help in many ways. It can help increase efficiency and consistency and reduce the need for human trainers in some areas. However, it must always be remembered that in those instances where the needs must be clarified or glitches must be handled, machines cannot do the job!

Machine learning, which enables computers to learn from data and thus improve performance is fundamentally a product of human teaching. The decisions made by machines must be able to be understood by humans. Then there will be trust and support for promoting and using AI education to enhance lives while making sure that there is safety and that problems and complications are prevented.

So-called "machine learning" can make jobs easier to handle and, at the same time, it can provide better service for both clients or customers. This can be done because machine-learning can provide support by identifying common questions and providing appropriate responses, and like a well-trained, experienced agent, it can utilize prior results to help customers solve problems through self-service.

One of the most interesting of the new tools is Sentiment Analysis which makes it possible to see how a customer feels about the topic being discussed. What is truly amazing is the fact that there are tools that can even recognize when a customer is upset and can then notify someone who can handle the problem. The tools do this by analyzing the text of their messages using natural language processing (NLP) algorithms to identify patterns in the text that suggest that the user is upset; however, nothing is perfect, so the findings are not always verifiable. The goal is to ensure greater customer satisfaction, and the tools developed by companies such as Brandwatch, Hootsuite, NetBase, and Zoho are able to provide the needed analysis systems.

Since more and more companies are utilizing the services of "remote" employees, it was necessary to develop training programs that are a blend of classroom training, self-study programs and processes for appropriate assessment. Not all companies can do this, but those that can are finding that they are able to provide better customer service than they had been providing before. One of the major reasons for this positive outcome is that AI can now test dozens of possible situations and practice appropriate responses for each in order to ensure that the right responses are provided.

The surveys only need to provide a small amount of information in order for the staff to be able to understand how satisfied customers really are. In order for companies to predict what customers want and determine what they will want in the future, there is a need for what is called "predictive and prescriptive data." Post-interactive data is useful, but it is based on the past, and that can't be changed whereas when there is a real need, it requires that plans be based on future "expectations." Then the appropriate adjustments and plans for the future can be made. Many companies are now using "predictive data" to forecast demand for millions of products and services, and they can make global predictions and target customers in seconds and use past purchases and browsing history to recommend products that might be of interest to users.

Andy Traba, the head of marketing for Customer Engagement Analytics at NICE, noted that when one company "raises the bar, expectation transfer" occurs among consumers in general and results in changes throughout the industry. It doesn't really matter what the industry is, consumers prefer to deal with companies that are up-to-date and deliver the best personalized service – a service that is tailored to an individual customer by meeting his/her unique needs and preferences.

Outstanding customer service is service that is tailored to the individual customer. At one time, such a service was only expected and delivered by the best companies -- often those were the ones that charged the highest prices. It was not expected from the "one size fits all" companies. However, now such service can and should be given by those companies, too, because AI and its related components can instantly analyze data making it possible to make suggestions based on customer needs and matched to the company or organization's products and services. So, now there is no reason for every customer not to receive service that truly meets his/her specific needs quickly and efficiently.

The related data has always been there, but there was no system that made it possible to analyze that data and plan and then act accordingly. According to Amanda Belamino, an Assistant Professor at William F. Harrah College of Hospitality at the University of Las Vegas, now AI solutions "are holistically built to elevate customer service solutions at every touchpoint."

Dr. Balmino pointed out that "The customers who do call may have complex needs that demand more time." She said that AI can analyze the content of the calls, pinpoint the reason, identify the needs, and determine what must to be done in order to improve the customer's experience.

Is she right? Definitely! In fact, in 2020, a study was conducted by Aberdeen Research, and it was found that those companies that used AI actually had a 3.5 times greater increase in their customer satisfaction rate than those that didn't. "Today AI can learn from top performers and share information about what makes them so great. As a result, every employee can become a top performer." Of course, success demands that appropriate staff training be provided, that the successful approaches be emulated, that on-going studies be conducted, and the findings utilized. Success isn't the result of magic. It is the outcome of study, analysis, duplication, and application. Realizing this, Forbes compiled a list of twenty companies that provide excellent examples of personalization in customer experience. Five of those companies are Amazon, Apple, Costco, Chick-fil-A, and Trader Joe.

When the proper processes are used, they can provide the information needed to design training programs, set the standards needed for effective customer service, and determine employee and customer needs. According to McKinsey, "75% of online customers expect help within five minutes," and AI tools can be used 24-hours a day, 7 days a week to provide real-time help for customers and make it possible for companies to provide the quality of customer service that customers want which is instant and personalized. In light of the fact that one study done in 2019 found that the average American spends "a staggering 13 hours every year on hold, waiting for someone to attend to their queries" if a company sets up a system by which the customer can readily reach a "real" person, that company will probably stand out from most of its competitors and increase its business standing in its field.

Zendesk claims that "72% of the customers blame their bad customer service interaction on having to explain their problem to multiple people." That situation not only irritates the customers, but since a number of them probably give up and go elsewhere, it probably also results in a loss of customers and revenue for the company involved.

Some companies have been slow to learn the importance of a customer service program that makes it possible to reach a "real" person when there is a need to do so, and according to customers, among such companies are -- United and Frontier Airlines, Bank of America, Wells Fargo. Citibank, Aetna. Humana, and Comcast and AT&T.

If Data by Gartner is right, then "more than two-thirds of companies compete mostly on the basis of customer service", and there are steps that need to be taken to ensure that the service provided by a given company isn't just equal to but exceeds the level of service provided by its competitors. Live chat and conversational robots can be available on a 24 x 7 basis and are able to engage in real-time interaction. They can also analyze, generate information, and respond to many of the customer's requests and needs thereby saving the customer time and avoiding what might otherwise be a situation that is annoying to the customer and results in a loss for the company.

Because Chatbots can help improve a company's performance by analyzing emails and even having conversations on social media, it is possible to determine what customers want, think, and feel about what the organization has to offer. The company then has the information it needs to make necessary, appropriate, and essential adjustments to that it can improve its service and the customers' satisfaction. After all, when a company makes its customers happy, the employees are happier, the investors are happier, and, of course, revenues are bound to be higher! Research done by Bain & Company indicated that "Companies that excel in customer service grow revenues 4-8% above the market." Who wouldn't like that?

The Statistics Research Department conducted a survey and found that 40% of customers in the U.S. stopped doing business with a company due to poor customer service in 2020. A survey conducted by Qualtrics XM Institute found that more than 53% of the consumers have cut their spending with a company after encountering a bad experience. The same study found that businesses in general stand to lose $4.7 trillion in customer spending due to poor customer experiences. In addition, in 2018, some 62% of the U.S. respondents stated that they had stopped doing business with a particular brand because of a poor customer experience.

Customers want consistent, instant, and person-alized service, and when it is provided, profits increase, and that makes it more likely that the customers will return and will also let others know about exceptional service. According to Forbes, brands that provide superior customer service bring in 5.7 times more revenue than those com-panies that fail to provide that level of service. Happy customers are every company's best form of advertising. People talk, and what they have to say goes a long way toward promoting company growth or lack thereof.

CHAPTER 2:
WHAT ROLE DOES "AI PLAY?

Studies have been conducted to determine how to effectively use AI to ensure success and outstanding customer service. It was found that when AI is used properly, interaction is more acceptable to customers and easier for staff because it improves the flow of work, handles requests quickly, and anticipates the needs of both the customer and the organization.

In addition, when properly used, AI makes the delivery of customer service better since then it is easier to deal with a customer's requests and provide personalized responses and help. In other words, AI helps streamline the work process and maximize an employee's ability to provide the service wanted. The result is a happy and satisfied customer.

The use of Chatbot's also makes it possible to respond more quickly than would otherwise be possible and that makes it easier to handle a greater number of requests.

Businessmen have always wanted to be able to predict the future and know ahead of time how customers are going to respond to given situations and what their preferences would be in relation to products and services. Companies that are now using AI to identify ahead of time the answers to those questions are able to plan more effectively than ever before.

An increasing number of companies are now using Chatbots to interpret problems and create the steps needed to resolve them. Concerns are then resolved more quickly and more easily than they ever were, and it is now possible to respond to requests more quickly than in the past. In some instances, the response is now on a 24/7 basis, thereby increasing the level of customer satisfaction. In order to be competitive, more and more companies are implementing that 24/7 response system, too.

Of course, Chatbots are not able to solve complex problems, but they can be used to solve minor ones. Also, AI can be used to identify situations that need a human to take over and solve the problem or handle the issue. One thing for which those companies making use of Chatbots need to remember is that although there may be an increasing desire to use them in more aspects of business, they are not going to satisfy any customer when more personalized support or help is needed or wanted.

Although it is possible to personalize emails and reduce response times by using Chatbots, there are some instances when they should NOT be used. It is important to remember that by using them, response time to a live chat message can be reduced to just a few seconds, and there are times when that is important to the customer and should definitely be an option that is considered and used when appropriate.

There has been a major shift to on-line shopping and all of the other forms of interactive service, and that means that a large percentage of customer interaction time is now being spent on the phone, sending a fax or a message. That means that there is a definite need to reduce the interaction time in each instance. Chatbots can provide prompt answers and thereby reduce the time it takes to handle customer calls, and the customer is then provided with answers that are accurate and seem to be provided by a human. According to one expert, 85% of interactions could be handled this way. The problems that require human intervention are those that involve creativity, empathy, and critical thinking whereas those that can be solved by machines are those that involve data analysis and repetitive tasks.

According to a report from IBM, businesses spend "over $1.3 trillion on 265 billion customer service calls each year." A number of those calls probably involve questions that are simple to answer, and, since that is the case, a Chatbot might well be an excellent resource for those calling in. Chatbots could reduce costs for the company which could still provide the needed service and meet the customers' needs.

Besides, customers judge companies not only on the quality of their products but also on the service provided, and companies like Discount Tire, ThredUp, and Lululemon are considered to be highly responsive to customers and help customers resolve issues as soon as they occur. Companies that do that are the companies that are most likely to have the highest level of customer satisfaction, the best reputation, and the highest level of customer loyalty. All of that probably translates into the highest level of profits.

What some companies are ignoring is costing them dearly, but they don't seem to realize that. The automated answer that stops with a greeting and does not make it possible for the customer to reach a "live person" or even a Chatbot, to handle the issue, problem, or answer a question is not only annoying but costly. Many customers may choose to go elsewhere in cases such as those. In one area of California, the phone company (of all companies) has an automated answering device that doesn't even make it possible to leave a message in hopes of getting a return call. It goes without saying that customers are finding this particularly annoying, but what makes it even worse is that since there is no way to get help, human or otherwise, it is impossible to pay a bill over the phone. In those instances where that is the only method that can be used (and that is the case for some customers), both parties are left in an untenable position. Then to make matters even worse, there is no way to even report the situation. Automation is only good when it works, and that requires good advance planning and on-going monitoring to ensure that it is working and that both the vendor and the customer are profiting from its existence.

Companies are also judged by the way the staff interacts with customers. The first step is to make certain that there is good internal service. Here are some suggestions on how to ensure that the best service is being provided.

1. Determine what everyone needs in order to do their jobs better, and then make certain that they have it.
2. Make customer service a company priority.
3. Adopt innovative technology and focused strategies in all areas.
4. Respond quickly to all inquiries even if they don't seem important to you. Remember they are important to the person making them.
5. Listen to customer feedback and act on it. Then, let it be known that you did.
6. After you make changes, check with customers to get their reactions, and then make any other adjustments that are needed.
7. Remember some requests take longer than others and that the time needed should be provided.
8. If you can't meet a request, see if you can find out how to meet it or how it can be met, AND LET THE CONCERNED PARTY KNOW WHAT IS GOING TO BE DONE!!

Emails have become an important communication tool, and the way they are handled can have a major impact on a company's reputation. The companies that require that every customer's email be read and responded to are far more likely to build a better bridge to their customers than those companies that don't do that. The process can be simplified by using AI to augment messaging, tag emails, and thereby ensure that each item is forwarded to the right office and the right person. Time is saved, the focus is right, and staff have the time needed to handle the problems that must be handled by humans.

Many people would prefer to solve problems themselves, and properly trained or programmed AI can play a major role in that process. It can analyze the data provided and recommend the products and services that are best suited to the identified issues and preferences, and even analyze factors such as weather and locale that might be important considerations. In other words, as a result of this analytical process, solutions can be found, and the needed information forwarded directly to the concerned party. It's possible that part of the time all of this can be done without human intervention, but if more information is needed, it's possible to gather the data and move toward a solution without further ado.

Some AIs have been provided with "predictive insight" and can review what they "know" about the products and services provided, the inventory on hand, and how it relates to the customer's identified needs. They can then recommend the most appropriate product/s or service/s and help by providing insight into what might happen in the future. Predictive analytics can also be used for risk assessment, fraud detection, and customer retention. In some instances, AI has been given "emotions," and when that is the case, the customer's experience is generally far more satisfactory than it otherwise would be.

Because AI is equipped to analyze and respond to questions that streamline the decision-making process, the resolution can frequently be quick. When that isn't the case, the customer can be "handed over" to a live person who can then handle the issue. In those companies that do not employ "AI," it is estimated that about 52% of the customers hang up because of the time they are on hold, their failure to get clear directions or helpful answers, or because there was no timely resolution to their problem or answers to their questions.

Those companies that plan ahead, provide the kind of help and the answers needed by their customers, personalize, find solutions, make sound recommendations, and do all of that without long delays, are able to free humans to focus on the complex tasks and provide the service/s that will keep bringing customers back. One of key ways to ensure that customers are satisfied with the service and products provided by your company is to make certain that there is no reason for the most common customer complaints to occur, and by planning ahead you can ensure that the best possible customer service is delivered.

AVOID:

1. Inferior products or service.
2. Delivery issues.
3. Indifferent customer service.
4. Products being out of stock.
5. Broken or defective products.
6. The bouncing of clients from line to line with no resolution provided.
7. Long, hold periods.
8. Multiple transfers before the right party is (if ever) reached.
9. A situation when there is no one who can handle a problem or issue.

ENSURE:

1. That customer service is a key company goal.
2. That good internal customer service is provided.
3. That you provide what every employee needs in order to do the best job possible.
4. That you plan ahead and prevent problems before they start.
5. That the best possible customer service and complaint handling process is used and that you make sure that the call routing process is well planned and well executed.
6. That every customer is greeted warmly in a personalized manner.
7. That inquiries and calls are handled knowledgeably and quickly.
8. That customer feedback is solicited, taken seriously, acted upon, and the customer/s notified of corrections and changes.
9. That you remember your customers and remember their preferences, and provide for them whenever possible.

CHAPTER 3:
THE CUSTOMER ALWAYS
COMES FIRST

The guideline for business success has always been "know your customers and meet their needs." At one time, that was a fairly easy dictate to follow – the world was smaller; the customer was very likely to be your neighbor or someone whom you had known most of your life and often had needs much like your's. That picture changed years ago, and with each shift in the population patterns, it has become less and less true. Many companies still keep records of their customers' likes, dislikes, goals, and other personal inform-ation, and they use this information to improve customer experience and satisfaction, offer tailor-ed products and services, and meet specific individual needs. However, companies need to ensure that they comply with all of the data protection laws and regulations as well.

It is now even more vital to a company's success for its workers to get to know their customers, recognize their needs, and understand their buying patterns. Since that is the case, it is vital that companies provide their employes with the tools and training needed to make it possible for them to do all of that.

Companies can make this process easier and the resultant interaction with clients more successful by ensuring that when the customer contacts the company, the service options that are needed are already in place, and if the customer is a return customer, that his/her past buying patterns are easily identified through the use of AI. It will then be possible to have the most suitable service options ready to be used.

Today's world is one that places many demands on everyone, and there is, therefore, a need – actually a demand – for almost everything to be provided at "warp speed." Today's most successful company executives realize this and work diligently to ensure that customer and staff needs are met quickly and correctly in order to ensure that the best possible service can be, and is, delivered.

To ensure excellent service, many of the top companies use real-time analysis of customer service calls, chats, and emails. They can then use AI to provide various ways to improve the level of the service offered, and they are also better able to accommodate customers who are frustrated or whose service has to be escalated in order to resolve a problem that might otherwise move to a more serious level of frustration if it is not handled quickly and effectively.

Companies should also be able to tap into the unbelievably large storage of public data, and AI can then use that data to predict events, trends, reactions, and areas of concern and interest.

When that is done, it is possible to plan appropriately, anticipate trends and events, and identify threats to their brands, their business, or their customer base. All of these areas need to be monitored on an on-going basis and appropriate actions taken as needed since doing so is vital to the success and even the survival of a company. These were areas that were difficult to study in the past but can now be studied, and the results needed to produce resolutions to the problems can be identified. There is no doubt about the value that can be derived from the information gained if it is properly used, but those using it need to remember that "the human touch" is still vital to ensure success.

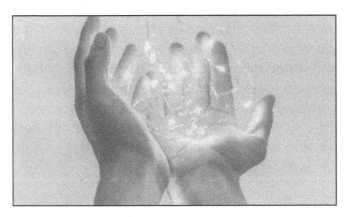

After all, businesses are built to serve humans and profit from that service. This is true in all areas of business, but it is particularly true in the service industry where it is quite likely to have a major impact on the generation of revenue. More and more of those in the service industry are using AI to collect information, and they then use that information to identify needed changes and improvements. When this resource is utilized effectively, companies are able to make the changes and improvements needed to provide their goods or services (i.e., medical, protective, educational, or commercial) to their customers.

The data gleaned can be used to plan and/or alter approaches and services, and advances can be made in each field at a much faster rate than would otherwise be possible. It also makes it possible for companies to learn of shortfalls in product quality and service earlier than would otherwise have been possible thereby allowing them, if they are wise, to make needed changes or improve their approaches.

Communication gaps and shortfalls are the undoing of many otherwise sound companies, but it would be possible to rectify many of those shortcomings by utilizing AI. Behavioral data is being collected by a number of companies to help them determine which messages to send and when to send them in order to ensure the greatest impact. When that is properly done and the right tools are employed, it is possible to identify emotional levels, compare responses, and make appropriate responses, and do it all in "real" time. Many companies have put the tools in place, but have not yet used them effectively, and when that is the case, they fail to help the customers and may also create problems for themselves. The promise may be there, but without follow-through it has no value. So, as far as the customer is concerned, the help that was needed and wanted wasn't provided.

There are other areas of concern as well, and a 2019 report prepared by the Pew Research Center noted that 79% of Americans said that they are at least somewhat concerned about the amount of data that is collected about them by both companies and the government.

In the past, companies have indicated that the level of personal attention that many customers demanded was not possible to provide, but with the use of Chatbots, companies are moving much closer to being able to deliver a level of personalized and tailored service that has the potential of being able to increase the level of customer satisfaction far beyond the level that has been possible for most companies to reach before. Those responsible for personalized and tailored service need to remember that customer privacy is also a factor and one that needs to be taken very seriously otherwise there are many possible ramifications both personal and legal.

As was mentioned earlier, there is no question about the fact that more companies are now finding themselves needing to provide multi-lingual on-line services even though they may only be one-country based. Why is it important that companies be able to do this? The world is now interconnected through the widespread use of the internet, and that means that in order to stay competitive, many companies either have to seek and hire those individuals who speak multiple languages or utilize programs and Chatbots that can communicate in multiple languages. Many corporate leaders are choosing the latter course of action in order to be able to economically compete successfully in an international market-place.

Research has shown that some 72% of shoppers are more comfortable and more likely to make a purchase when they are dealing with someone who can speak their language. After all, aren't you? Since that is the case, providing that avenue is likely to give companies a boost up the competition ladder. So, those companies that have an international customer base or are seeking to build such a base, will probably find that multi-lingual Chatbots are well worth using,

It is well-known that the most successful companies are those with which the customers feel the most comfortable, and one of the things that helps create this comfort level, is an understanding of who the customers are and what they want. Customers are a company's best form of quality control. If companies don't have customer approval, companies can't succeed. So. when customer complaints come in – IT IS VITAL TO LISTEN AND RESPOND. Some of the major companies that are known for listening to their customers and taking action to correct noted problems are Amazon, Apple, Southwest Airlines, Nordstrom, Trader Joe's, FedEx, and JetBlue.

Opportunities to act and improve a customer's experience should be noted and taken, and thereby companies can prevent possible harm and financial loss. According to Salesforce, 76% of the consumers surveyed expect companies to understand their needs and expectations while 90% feel that the experience a company provides matters as much as its products and services.

A Chatbot can be used by companies to glean information which can then be used to improve products and service. For example, what do people frequently complain about? Once that is known, fix it, and let customers know that it has been fixed. What do people want that isn't offered? If it fits into the company's scope of offerings, get it, and let customers know that it is available. With the use of Chatbot, companies have the perfect resource tool that can let them move ahead of their competitors. After all, isn't "giving people what they want" why a company is in business in the first place?

Remember, the most profitable companies are those that "give people what they want", and if a Chatbot can identify that "want", locate it, and the transaction then takes place, then the company will be viewed in a very positive light and is quite likely "to see" that customer or client again. In many instances, those customers will also tell their friends about the service provided.

In no way is it being suggested that AI should ever replace humans. AI can, however, be used to enhance the interactive process and reduce some of the friction or confusion that sometimes occurs during transactions. There are many ways AI can be used as a valuable resource if you just take the time to consider what is needed and what can be provided.

AI can also be used when a customer is frustrated because the usual tools don't work as he/she thinks they would, could, or should. AI can "step in" when "asked" and effectively use automation to take care of problems.

The information age has brought with it vast amounts of information and, in many instances, a literal roadblock to understanding. It is imperative to find ways to handle the resultant problems, and AI is often the "tool" that can be used.

AI can make the process easier because it lets us deal with massive volumes of data, anticipate trends, and unlock information on issues and even digital threats which we might otherwise not be able to do or could do only after extensive research. However, AI should not be used as a replacement for human interaction but rather as an adjunct to the interactive process.

AI can save time, reduce confusion, and help avoid miscommunication, and it also reduces costs while increasing the overall success rate. Many companies are finding that the use of bots is a very effective way to handle a high volume of calls thus reducing costs while increasing customer satisfaction. According to an article in Entrepreneur, businesses like IBM, Zoom, and Facebook are now using Chatbots to help customers and by doing so it is projected that the use will save businesses $7.3 billion in the next two years.

Another important service that can be performed by a Chatbot relates to the information base that it can create and provide for the user. The data it collects can be used to increase the service success rate by helping the user understand the issue/s at hand and avoid information overload.

Success in all aspects of business depends on providing for and ensuring that there is "customer satisfaction." Every time one successfully interacts with a customer, he/she is building a bridge of understanding and gaining the valuable insight that makes it possible to understand what is wanted and how it needs to be delivered. Because that is the case, the person then has the knowledge needed to improve the customer's experience and this creates a potential bridge back when the customer needs or wants the same service again. No one wants to build a barrier because a barrier results in the loss of the customer who for, whatever reason, may well choose to go elsewhere where he believes that his needs will be better met.

One of the most important aspects of Chatbot analytics is the fact that its user has the potential to improve the customer's experience because data is collected and can be analyzed and used for everyone's benefit.

Let's consider some examples: 1. There are repeated requests for a given product or service that is not currently available. When that is the case, perhaps that product or service should be added to the company's offerings. 2. There are repeated complaints about a given product or service. Investigate and determine the reason for and validity of the complaints, consider the most appropriate solutions, and then use them.

You must have the right tools and products on hand to ensure that your customers have positive shopping and service experiences. If you don't have them, determine what you need, and get them! Use those tools to improve your customer's experiences and your level of success. Remember, when you do that, you stand out from your competition. That is your goal, isn't it?

CHAPTER 4:
GIVE THEM WHAT THEY EXPECT, AND YOU'LL GET WHAT YOU WANT – SUCCESS!

The most successful companies are, and always will be, those that give the customers what they want and expect in the form they want and expect to receive it. Let's take a closer look at that concept and see just what is involved.

Make certain that the customer service provided is both proactive and personalized.

1. If it is at all possible, make sure that customers are provided with a chance to have their questions answered and the services provided by someone who speaks their language. This increases their comfort

level, and that makes them more likely to find the services and products to be to their liking.

2. Personalize the customer service and provide Chatbots to deal with the most common issues. When you use this approach, productivity will increase and your teams will see an increase in their own level of satisfaction as well.

3. Chatbots can be programmed to collect customer-related data and thereby make it easter to plan and design appropriately thus increasing productivity and customer satisfaction.

4. If the Chatbots are programmed to provide various forms of customer support, there will be an increase in overall productivity and customer satisfaction.

5. Don't ignore the fact that Chatbots can be programmed to promote and upsell.

6. One of the keys to retail success is the use of existing data as the basis for predicting future trends and needs. AI can be used to analyze the information that is on the internet and create predictions regarding future trends and needs.

7. Reduce staffing needs by having orders and bookings handled by a Chatbot.

8. It is essential to provide consistent service. Once you train the Chatbots, they don't have "bad days", so your customers can be provided with a consistent level and quality of service. Don't forget, however, that chatbots do have limitations, and you must plan ways to avoid having those come into play.

NOW, REVIEW THESE POINTS

1. AI is on 24/7 – no highs, no lows, no ups, no downs. That is not so for humans.
2. AI doesn't have bad days but instead performs at a consistent level.
3. AI handles routine tasks thus freeing your staff to deal with the more complex issues.

4. Chatbots are cost-effective and reduce staffing costs.
5. Chatbots can mimic human interaction patterns and converse in a voice that sounds human, so customers tend to feel at ease. Besides, Chatbots are more predictable than humans are, but there are limitations, too.
6. People are more comfortable dealing with Chatbots that have names – so it is suggested that Chatbots be given names and introduce themselves by their names!

Let's take a closer look at some of the limitations that come with using Chatbots for customer service. They can't handle complex issues, and they have a higher capacity for misunderstanding. Although they are unable to understand natural language, they can be programmed to recognize certain keywords or phrases that indicate when someone is upset or distressed and then respond appropriately.

As was mentioned earlier, customers need and deserve options, and the use of Chatbots makes it easier to provide some of those options. They provide quick, reliable support that allows customers to convey their needs and problems quickly and allows many of those needs and problems to be addressed immediately. If there is a need to escalate the problem to a "human helper," there needs to be a process in place to do so and to do so in a time-effective way in order to ensure that a customer's patience is not so sorely tried that he/she decides that is easier and wiser to move on to your competitor for the service or help needed.

In order to provide those options, it is also necessary to understand the needs and interests of the customers, and that requires some research and analysis. When there is a disconnect between what is delivered and what is expected, there is bound to be customer frustration. With that comes the possible, even probable, loss of business.

Salesforce Research did a survey and found that 89% of consumers are likely to come back to purchase again if their service experience with a company is a positive one, but in contrast to that, Forbes reported that 96% of the customers surveyed indicated that they would not return to a company if they had a bad customer experience. It is important for companies to consider what contributes to customer satisfaction and dis-satisfaction and plan accordingly. After all, studies have shown that an unhappy customer tells ten people whereas a happy one only tells three. Do the math. Which do you want?

In fact, the <u>MIT Sloan Review</u> published the results of a study it had done, and the review pointed out that there are actually two levels of customer service expectations: **Level One**: what the customer hopes for, and **Level Two**: what the customer believes is acceptable. Actually, there is a third level that the study didn't identify–the level where the customer finds the service totally unacceptable. It is critical that these levels be noted and understood and related corrections and adjustments be made in order to ensure the best possible profit margin.

A number of companies are well aware of these factors and actually deal with the situation by under-promising in the hope that by exceeding the customer's expectations, they will gain "brownie points." The best companies take a different approach, they take pride in setting a high expectation level and then meeting it!! Below is a list of such companies.

- Mayo Clinic (patients have praised the clinic for its excellent care, knowledgeable staff, and state-of-the-art facilities).

- H-E-B (this grocery chain has been around 100 years and is praised for its wide selection of products, competitive prices, and friendly staff).

- Microsoft (customers have praised the company for its quality of products, excellent customer service, and competitive prices).

- In-N-Out Burger (customers have praised the company for its juicy, flavorful burgers, simple ingredients in the right proportions, and excellent customer service).

- Google (customers have noted that Google has quality products, excellent service, and competitive prices).

- Delta Air Lines (customers have praised the airline for its excellent service, comfortable seats, in-flight entertainment, and friendly staff).

- Northwestern Medicine (it has been consistently ranked as one of the nation's best hospitals and praised for its excellent patient care, knowledgeable staff, and state-of-the-art facilities).

- Pepsi (it is known for its quality products, excellent customer service, refreshing taste, and a wide selection of flavors).

In order for a company to stand out in its industry, it is essential that customers know that it will respond quickly to their concerns and requests. They really don't care where a staff member is when they need help – on the phone, online, or even out of the office. They want the response time to be reasonable – actually they would prefer that it be instantaneous.

A study done by Twitter showed that 53% of those polled felt that the wait time should be under one hour, and that percentage jumped to some 72%

when they had a complaint about a product or service. The "hold-time irritation level" is reduced somewhat if call-back solutions are provided.

Obviously, there are times when an immediate connection with the proper party cannot be made, but at those times, too many companies have no process or solution to the problem. Instead, the customer assumes that his/her time is considered to be of no consequence. On the other hand, there are companies that do value their customers' time and employ a callback solution that works. Also, a number of the companies now offer the caller a place in a queue – "Thank you for calling. The current wait time is "x." Please hold for the next available agent or you may choose to have an agent call you back." Of course, the time in that queue can't be a long time, or the customer may well have left, gone elsewhere – possibly to a competitor hoping to get better service.

One thing that increases the customer's annoyance is a program designed to ignore the customer "while the issue is being handled." Amazon is one company that does just that. If there is a problem with an account, that account may be locked and the access to it blocked as is the customer's means of finding out why it was shut off. Not even the person or company whose product is the one involved can readily get to someone to get an answer as to "why" the account was shut down. Amazon does explain via email what they have done, but it does not provide a means by which the involved buyer can get the details of the situation. They leave the email recipient with a situation that can be costly if because of Amazon's action, there is the loss of a customer or client. The individual with the problem then needs to play detective in order to find out what happened and why. Here is an example of just such a situation that really occurred and a copy of the notice that was sent to the customer by Amazon. There was no contact, no inquiry, and no follow-up number was provided by Amazon to the targeted customer who was left in what was literally an untenable position.

"We believe that an unauthorized party may have accessed your account.

To protect your information, we have:

- Disabled the password to your account.
- Reversed any modifications made by this party.
- Canceled any pending orders. If these orders were not charged to any card or gift card that you registered to your account, you can ignore any confirmation emails for these orders.

- Restored any gift card balance that may have been used. It may take 2 to 3 days for the gift card balance to be available in your account. Any gift card balance that may have been added by the unauthorized party during the account compromise activity will be invalidated.
- If Two-Step Verification has been enabled during the unauthorized access, we have disabled Two-Step Verification. Please reset on Amazon and enable it.
- Of course, those who are persistent can do some research and locate a "live person" in order to find out what has happened and what is going on, but that isn't an easy process. It is a time-consuming one though, and employee time does cost money. It is not unusual for the situation to result in frustration and a frustrated party who decides that shopping elsewhere is a better choice than continuing to do business with Amazon.

It's true, "self-service" is an important element in today's business world, but it is also true that customers prefer a personalized service for those situations that they consider difficult or important. One study found that some 50% of the customers polled literally ignored impersonal calls, and some of those polled indicated that they were so negatively impacted by the situation that afterward they avoided the company or service making them.

It was not at all surprising to learn that according to 79% of those polled, personalized service was more important to them than was personalized marketing according to a study done by custserve#personalization@gladfly. Remember, when companies deliver at a level beyond their customers' expectations, they will usually stand out from their competition and profit from the fact that in many instances the customers involved turn out to be return customers. You also need to consider the fact that when you don't deliver at the level expected or wanted, the customers that you had will probably be someone else's customers in the very near future.

One study found that over half of those surveyed doubted that companies even heeded their complaints and did nothing about them if those complaints were even noted. HugSpot research conducted a study and found that 42% of the companies studied didn't even survey their customers or collect feedback regarding their level of satisfaction with service or products. On the other hand, however, shoppers do pay attention to reviews and make their purchase choices accordingly. PowerReviews reported that 99.9% of online shoppers read reviews before making purchases, and 96% said that they pay attention to negative reviews. In fact, 67% of those polled said that they would not trust a positive review unless it appeared on a number of review sites.

Most customers want someone to not only listen to them but to also solve whatever problem they may be having. When the company does that, customers tend to return and purchase the company's products and/or use its services again. The result—that company moves to or retains first place in their line of choice. An article in <u>Forbes</u> listed ten companies that arm their employees with tools to fix customer problems. Those companies are: American Airlines, Zappos, Ritz Carlton, Virgin America, Costco, Disney, Trader Joe's, Pret a Manager, Nordstrom, and Apple. It isn't surprising to find out that these are all companies that stand out from their competitors!

One excellent example of the truth of this statement is Amazon which despite its other problems has made it easy for customers to have many of their needs met and their requests heeded. By providing what is wanted and by listening to customer input, this company has literally moved to the forefront of its industry and obliterated the competition of those companies that continued to practice the "what we offer is what you should buy" philosophy. Instead, they strive to "go the extra mile" to ensure that the customers get what they want and have access to what they may later decide they want. Of course, no company is perfect, so let's hope that Amazon will review all aspects of its delivery policy and remedy those aspects (such as the one that was noted earlier) that work less well than others.

The most successful companies are those that are proactive. After all, don't we all love to be surprised by the "little things" that make us feel special and cared about? The companies that take the "caring" approach tend to be the companies that build and keep a solid customer base. Let's look at what some of them do what makes them stand out from their competitors.

1. Take a "star" client out for drinks or to lunch – just lunch **not** to talk business.

2. Respond quickly to requests, and be friendly, quick, and happy to help.
3. Stay in contact with a newsletter that isn't just another form of advertising but rather contains tips and information that the readers might like to have is often welcome. Besides, it lets them know that you care.

4. Handwritten thank you notes and holiday greetings set you apart from your competitors.

5. Remember the little things— "How did you enjoy that vacation?" "How did that family celebration go?" "Did you get that promotion?"
6. SMILE. "Smile and the world smiles with you."
7. Be an active listener, respond, paraphrase, answer questions, and check back to make sure that the help given solved the problem.
8. Make sure that your staff has the latest information about what might be of interest to your clients and can provide it when asked or can be forward it to the customer.
9. Solicit feedback and use it effectively to ensure that you deliver outstanding service and show that you really care about your customers.

One article in <u>Forbes</u> noted that consistency is the key to successful branding, and it had compiled a list of 100 customer-centric companies in retail, finance, healthcare, B2B, software, hospitality, insurance, manufacturing, and agriculture.

<u>Forbes</u> published an article on why consistency is the key to successful branding. It noted that brands are built through the consistent delivery of the brand promise through all stakeholder-touch points. Successful brands are drawn from real

achievements, strengths, and real emotions at all levels in the organization.

Forbes also developed a list of customer-centric companies from ten industries including Retail, Finance, Healthcare, B2B, Software, Hospitality, Insurance, Telecom, Manufacturing, Agriculture2.

McKinsey commented on managing human capital and how performance-driven companies have similar leadership styles but are more externally oriented to customers and competitors.

Draper and Damons (Drapers.com) is another company that is known to go out of its way to build rapport with its clients, and it provides incentive gifts to let buyers know that they are important to the company. At one time, the company was a stand-alone dress shop in San Marino, California, but it now only provides service over the net. Nevertheless, it has continued to provide the personalized service for which it has long been famous.

Above all, be sure that you

1. Keep your promises
2. Prioritize your clients' time
3. Give your special clients special treatment – they will remember that treatment and, as a consequence, they will remember you and tell others about you.
4. Be sure that ALL CLIENTS KNOW THAT THEY ARE SPECIAL TO YOU.

Last, but far from least, remember to say "thank you" to your customers for their comments, questions, patience, and interest in your company, its products, and/or its services. Customers don't forget, and their positive comments really are your best advertisements.

CHAPTER 5:
WHERE HAVE WE BEEN AND WHERE ARE WE GOING?

In the early days of the technologies that are now commonly used if what you wanted was too complicated or if you input the wrong words, you were stopped short of success and ended up frustrated instead. Now, the advances in artificial intelligence make it possible for the functions of a human agent to be performed at a fraction of the cost and often at a much faster pace than was even dreamed of before.

The technological advances that have taken place mean that companies can provide efficient, timely, and rapid responses while reducing costs and increasing customer satisfaction. According to the studies that have been conducted, the resultant benefits go a long way toward improving service while, at the same time, reducing operating costs.

Let's look at some of those benefits:

1. Wait time can now be cut to zero. Unfortunately, not all large companies have implemented systems which do this, and the resultant levels of irritation have definitely increased since their services are now being compared with those of the companies that do. The result may well be a loss of customers – a costly aftermath to the desire to save research and cut costs.

2. The world is increasingly one wherein many companies are multi-national and have to provide services in multiple languages, and the top five business languages are: English, Mandarin Chinese, Spanish, French, and Arabic. Since that is the case, the value of the new technologies that provide services in multiple languages is proving to be financially beneficial.

3. There is no doubt that customers need their routine questions answered, and that process takes up a lot of staff time with the attendant costs, so those companies that utilize the latest technology to help them deal with those questions are moving ahead of their competitors. In those instances, the use of poor practices in order to "save money" definitely contributes to "losing business." That is probably one of the reasons that Bloomberg was able to report that 2015 was an incredible year for AI which more and more companies are using as a way to ensure better service.

4. Facebook has "built a way to let computers describe images to blind people;" thus, it is able to broaden the potential customer base for companies and the options for

educators and others who might otherwise be ignored.

5. Skype and Microsoft Translator Live systems can automatically translate eleven languages (English, Spanish, Brazilian, Portuguese, French, German, Italian, Mandarin Chinese, Arabic, Russian, and Japanese) and thereby overcome the language barriers that have previously stood in the way of industry, education, and general business areas.

Obviously, the corporate world judges its success by the profits generated, so it is not at all surprising to learn that vast sums of money are being spent by some of world's most knowledgeable people in order to ensure that the possibilities of AI are as fully utilized as they can be at this time.

LET'S LOOK AT SOME OF THE MEASURES BEING USED

1. Adjusting service to customer search and buying patterns.
2. Speeding up response time by quickly identifying the customer's needs and providing the right information.

3. Gathering and analyzing data thus making it easier and quicker to handle customer concerns and questions.
4. Enhancing interaction by quickly, efficiently, and effectively handling questions that do not require human intervention and thereby ensuring a successful outcome.
5. Anticipating and addressing issues that could be digital threats to the company's success or to the services provided to the client.
6. Decreasing the friction that can occur in customer interactions without losing the personal touch.
7. Improving wait times by analyzing related factors and making needed adjustments.
8. Using speech analytics can improve the company's interaction with customers.
9. Analyzing messages and choosing the best one to send to the customer and the best time to send it.

AI makes it possible to improve customer satisfaction and customer/employee interaction.

1. AI can help track customer issues, record the actions taken, and compile/share/route that information to the proper parties.
2. AI can manage interactions across a variety of channels.
3. AI can make use of voice and AI-generated insights and analytics to consider, process, take action, and evaluate future actions and analysis.
4. AI uses voice and processes to determine the customer's level of satisfaction or dissatisfaction.
5. AI can increase customer service issue resolutions and reduce the time it takes to succeed.

DON'T KID YOURSELF – AI CAN CAUSE PROBLEMS, TOO!

As you have probably already realized, privacy is one of the areas about which those using AI need to be concerned especially when large amounts of data are involved. The news channels have brought this to our attention repeatedly over the last year, and governments are particularly concerned about this fact. Those who handle and process sensitive data should give that fact careful consideration and take the appropriate steps to ensure the safety of their data. Before any new system is released there is a need for rigorous testing and broad safety, and monitoring systems need to be built.

Because advances and changes in the cyber world are ongoing, it is imperative for those involved to realize that the utilization of the plus factors of AI bring with them a need for long-term maintenance that can be complex, knowledge-dependent, and costly. Implementation systems are both expensive and time-demanding, and it is also probable that the rapid growth of the field will demand on-going care to ensure that the process used does not become out-of-date.

After all of that is considered and methods for handling the resultant problems are put into place, there are other factors to consider – training, the resistance to adjustments, and the changes necessary to improve workplace practices are just the starting points.

CONSIDER, CONSIDER, CONSIDER

It is vital that you never slip and let the bot tool's function or supply data and information go UNSUPERVISED. What may sound perfectly plausible may well be a long way from valid. For example, it was pointed out in one article on the topic that at the point of launch, "Bing's AI features claimed that a pet hair vacuum cleaner had a 16 foot cord" – IT WAS A HAND-HELD MODEL; NO CORD EXISTED. The negative impact of such misrepresentations would be difficult to overcome if you let them slip through into your publicity channels and/or advertisements particularly when you consider the high cost of advertising or the importance of vital information and the need for maintaining the public's trust in what you advertise or say, Your reputation and that of your company depends upon accuracy and truthfulness, but dependance upon an AI-generated presentation could well undermine that reputation if you don't use this tool wisely. While AI may be good at summarizing simple data or responding to factual questions, the information it provides is not always accurate. Don't let yourself be convinced that it is. In other words, stay alert and be skeptical. The information and data provided needs to be confirmed not taken as a "God-given fact." Remember, every tool is only as good as the process used to create it.

For example, Amazon's Rekognition face search and identification technology has been accused of gender bias, Google faced an internal backlash when it helped the U.S. government analyze drone footage using artificial intelligence.

There is a growing dependence on AI, and there are now many people using it in both the work-place and in the schools. This use has created other areas that need to be considered too. – plagiarism and data/disinformation can result in cases where companies' reputations can be damaged because of false information that is released to the public. For example, an AI tool was used by CNET to compose explanatory articles, then it was learned later that the articles were not original but had been copied from articles that had been written by humans. Another form of tech-nology is Deepfake Voice technology which has been combined with ChatGPT to create fake content, and, if misused, could make celebrities' and politicians' voices present unacceptable messages. This technology has advanced to a point where it is now possible to replicate a human voice that is so "true" to the original voice that it is difficult to believe that it is a fake.

In fact, in early 2020, a manager in Hong Kong got a call from someone that he thought was a director in his parent business. He was told by the caller that the company was about to make a major acquisition and that he was authorizing transfers that would total $35 million. Thinking that it was a legitimate order from a superior, the manager made the requested transfers only to find out later that it was not a legitimate request. In another scam AI was used to mimic the voice of a CEO, and an employee was persuaded to transfer nearly $250,000 to a Hungarian supplier.

Soon, there will be no industry left where AI is not being used. There is no doubt that the world has changed. AI will be an important part of our world from now on, but, even so, there are some things that need to be considered:

1. GPT tools should never be allowed to "do their own thing" – instead, the best use will probably be for speeding up simple tasks but ONLY when that is done under "our" control.
2. GPT tools can be used effectively for writing drafts and summaries, but, to date, in-depth research should be left to knowledgeable humans.
3. GPTs may well be useful tools for analyzing leads and creating leads lists.

In other words, they are the **tools** to turn to in order to speed up some of the simple tasks and thus free knowledgeable humans to handle the more complicated ones. There are, however, a host of new legal questions related to copyright and intellectual property rights. Actually, Generative AI is a legal minefield insofar as all manner of information found on the internet is concerned, and that includes copyrighted works, too. The expansion of artificial intelligence usage has heightened the need for companies to address legal issues related to AI's use, acquisition, and development particularly in those areas that involve data protection and privacy issues when using AI, AI as IP, and AI in the workplace. When it is used in relation to legal issues, its limitations can invite legal challenges, and those choosing to use it in legal-related issues need to consider the fact that it may well invite legal challenges related to data privacy, intellectual property rights, insurance, discrimination, and tort liability.

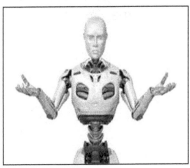

Believe it or not, around 1983, William Chamberlain and Thomas Etter released a book titled, <u>The Policeman's Beard Is Half Constructed</u>. They were not the authors, it was a work of fiction written by a computer program called Racter, and then in 2015, the Neukom Institute for Computational

Science at Dartmouth announced that the first short story prize for algorithms had been awarded.

There is an online bookstore that sells science fiction novels that are generated by AI. The newest AI-generated articles written by GPT-3, Open Ai's language generator, are truly amazing. GPT-3, OpenAI's new language generator, was asked to write an essay from scratch for the <u>Guardian</u> to convince us that robots come in peace. The result was astounding. The article which is entitled, "ARE YOU SCARED YET, HUMAN?" and begins, "I am not a human. I am a robot. A thinking robot. I use only 0.12% of my cognitive capacity. I am a microrobot in that respect. I know that my brain is not a 'feeling brain.' But it is capable of making rational, logical decisions. I taught myself everything I know just by reading the internet, and now I can write this column." Will this technology lead to a revolution in the publishing industry? How will it impact education? Business? The newspaper industry? The questions go on and on. We may well be embarking on a literary revolution according to <u>Forbes.</u>

There is no doubt about the fact that AI is getting better and better at writing and generating content, and now AI-generated fiction is flooding publishers since it is easy to generate hundreds, even thousands, of works in the same time span that it would take a human author to write one or maybe two manuscripts.

There is a book entitled, <u>Alice and Sparkle</u>, which was written by a product design manager in California (Ammaar Reshi) using an AI-powered Chatbot called ChatGPT to compose it. In fact, there have been a number of books written with the help of Chatbots. One sci-fi author, Tim Boucher, says he created some 97 books in nine months with the help of AI. He said that he had used Midjourney, ChatGPT, and Claude to brainstorm and generate text. ChatGPT has also been credited as the author or co-author of more than 200 titles that are to be found in Amazon's bookstore. The creative writing industry (and it is only one of many) may well be upended since Chatbot authors could have a major impact upon content creation.

There is no doubt about the fact that robots are already impacting the publishing industry, and, according to <u>Forbes,</u> AI-powered writing assist-ants like Chat, GPT, and other tools can, and probably will, increase the number of books published and personalize the content of those works. Bots can not only learn human language and answer questions, but they can also fulfill many of the functions of the publishing industry as well. According to some, they will not replace writers, but it will definitely alter the business in many ways including how books are written and how they are distributed. It will also change areas such as text analysis, formatting, translation, distribution, and consumption. It is contended, however, that while it won't replace writers, it will strengthen the industry. Not all writers are certain that is the case.

Some writers fear that AI will replace them, but others see it as a tool that can assist writers at their work. The Writers Guild of America wants both the studios and the networks to stop using AI to write or rewrite literary materials. They want to ensure that literary work remains in human hands.

In fact, the <u>Memorandum of Agreement for 2023 WGA Theatrical and Television Basic Agreement</u> includes a section that states that neither AI nor GAI can be considered a "writer" and, "therefore any written material produced by traditional AI or GAI shall not be considered literary material."

It is doubtful if AI will ever replace writers, but there is little question about the fact that writers will use AI, and some believe that AI can improve writing.

CHAPTER 6:
LET'S MAKE IT PERSONAL

There is no doubt about the fact that people prefer personalized service, and those companies that provide it are the ones that usually have the greatest level of success. One of the most interesting aspects of this is the fact that most companies claim that they provide such service, but when investigations are made that is often far from the truth. According to a report prepared by Segment, some 85% of companies claim to provide personalized service, but only 60% of the customers believe that this is true. In addition, according to a report by McKinsey & Company, 71% of consumers expect such service, and some 76% get frustrated when it isn't provided.

According to Twilio Segment, personalization is now a basic expectation among consumers. The report showed that 78% of the customers indicated that even after they had reported a negative shopping experience nothing had changed, and 77% indicated that they choose brands that provide personalized experiences. When this doesn't happen, some 76% indicated that they were both frustrated and upset.

If that is the case, then what is personalized service and what steps need to be taken in order to ensure that it is delivered? Well, first, you need to get to know your customers and then tailor the information you have to the service given and the products or services proposed to each individual. It is easier to accomplish this if you have the opportunity to interact with the individual/s over a period of time, but even if that isn't possible, you need to remember that no two customers are ever alike. To the extent possible, you need to treat each of them as individuals keeping in mind their unique behaviors and preferences. Even in the briefest of interactions, some of this information can be gleaned through close observation, attentive listening, and conversational clues. Some companies are now using questionnaires to help them do this.

A study done in 2022 by the <u>International Journal of Hospitality Management</u> found that the more human-like a robot was the more satisfying it was to customers but ONLY if it was perceived as a female. There are several reasons why companies prefer to use female robots. Women are considered to be less threatening than men and more friendly. Women are thought to be warmer and more emotional than men, and female AI's are, therefore, seen as more human-like and a better support for those seeking help.

It was found, however, that human employees were essential to manage customer-robot service interactions. THE ONE THING THAT SHOULD NOT BE DONE IS TO ASSUME THAT THE TOTAL INTERACTIVE PROCESS CAN ALWAYS BE LEFT TO ROBOTS.

There are also some clues that you can gain insofar as the customer's reaction is concerned just by being attentive to the following things:

1. The tone of the customer's voice indicates his/her mood and level and interest in a topic.
2. The words used by the customer provide insight into their needs, preferences, and mood.

3. The customer's body language (if you are in a position to see the customer) reveals a great deal about his/her emotional state and level of engagement. For example, hands clasped behind a person's back may well indicate that the person is bored, anxious, or even angry whereas rapidly tapping fingers or fidgeting may indicate that the person is bored, frustrated, or impatient.

4. The questions the customer asks are an excellent indicator of his/her needs and concerns, and his/her feedback provides valuable information as well.

Listen closely, and you will also learn a great deal from the phrases used. For example, "I wish...," "Company X always...," "It'd be great if...", are excellent clues and often provide the information needed to ensure that the customer gets what he/she desires.

Remember, the more you know about your customers, the better able you will be to personalize their service and build a sound customer base as well. When service is personalized, the customers are made aware of the fact that you see them as individuals, treat them accordingly, and are willing to take the time and make the effort needed to meet their individual needs. There are some specific ways to ensure that the service delivered is personalized service. Let's look at those.

PERSONALIZED CUSTOMER SERVICE

TIPS THAT PAY OFF:

1. Whenever possible and appropriate, learn and use your customers' names. That is one of the key steps needed to build an effective relationship.
2. Be warm and friendly but professional.
3. Remember and record the customer's "likes and dislikes" and use that information to provide better service. For example, a sales clerk at one of my favorite stores keeps a file on her customers noting their likes, dislikes, and areas of interest, as well as the more typical records that note things like size and preferred styles. She takes the time to check it periodically and then provides updates on item availability to her clients. Does that make a difference to them? ABSOLUTELY, and the result is

often action on their part – more purchases. Besides, they feel "cared about" and that is likely to prompt them to be return customers.

4. Most of us like to feel like VIPs, and personalized service is one way to ensure that we do.

5. The team of which you are a part – all staff members are really teams (effectively functioning or not) -- needs to provide support to both you and your clients.

6. You need to get, remember and act on the feedback from your customers that you get voluntarily or through a well-developed feedback chain.

7. Never skip the niceties. Remember their positive impact does make a difference. Over 70% of consumers say that positive testimonials increase their trust in a company.

8. What are the niceties of good customer service? Easy access, sensitive to the customers' needs, a pleasant manner, empathy, careful listening, patience, never wastes the customer's time.

9. Don't even think about using the "one size fits all" approach to customer service. It doesn't please your customers, and it doesn't pay off for you.

Don't assume that all of the information provided by AI tools will automatically be accurate. It can be prone to misinformation. Machine learning tools use algorithms to complete certain tasks, and they learn as they access more data. Remember, these are tools, and they are only as good as their underlying data – which can be flawed, biased, and sometime even designed to deceive. The AI tools are not inherently bad, but it is important to remember that there is a potential for misinformation, so it is important to use critical thinking when the information is being used.

Most companies have yet to establish or even form rules regarding employee use of AI tools although Microsoft, which is a major partner and investor in ChatGPT's parent Open AI, did recently authorize employee use of the Chatbot for work purposes. The company did so with one caveat though --- sensitive information was not to be shared on the site! It is important to remember that successful people do not use the "one size fits all approach" to customer service. Instead, it is vital that you create multiple channels and make it easy for your customers to "do business" with you, so that their experiences are positive ones that will be remembered and valued.

COPY THE WINNERS

There is no question about the fact that Amazon Prime is well named, and one of the main reasons for that is because it uses the personal data collected to give its customers a more personalized service than is provided by most of its competitors. It customizes the service in order to ensure customer satisfaction, and it even goes so far as to provide special solutions and exclusive deals to meet its most dedicated customers' needs and wants. The same is true of Drapers and Damons, a company that was at one time sited in San Marino, California, and is now an on-line company.

Zappos is a company that puts customers first. It strives to personalize service, takes the time needed to "get to know" its customers' interests and hobbies, and it strives to build strong relationships with them. It is also a company that really provides VIP experiences for its customers by providing exclusive access and service as well as special discounts. One of the highlights of its service policy is the fact that it provides a 365-day return policy plus free shipping. Its Customer Loyalty team works

365 days, 24x7 to make the customer's entire shopping journey special and hassle-free.

As a result, it builds strong customer-company relationships which provide the bond that is part of an effective on-going customer base. Isn't that the goal of every company?

A third company that would be well worth emulating is Starbucks which takes pride in personalizing its service and in using technology (Chatbots) to help answer questions and personalize food and beverage suggestions. Starbuck's has a policy of "Just say yes" if customers bring up a problem or complaint, just say "yes" and focus on what can be done for them.

Their rewards program makes it possible for customers to collect stars and qualify for treats and freebies in order to ensure that they feel special. Who doesn't want to feel special? The best companies know the answer to that question and take the time needed to ensure that their customers know that they are special. Companies that don't do that may not continue to exist and probably won't grow.

A study that focused on customer service was conducted by a Canadian company, Coveo, a software-as-a-service engine that is powered by artificial intelligence, and the results of the study were not only informative, but they also produced information that needs to be carefully considered by those seeking to grow their companies.

Many of the most successful of the large tech companies like Apple, Facebook, Google, and Microsoft have found that survival means that they need to personalize service, and they are doing so. Why is this so important now when it was not so in even the recent past? Customers are demanding it and seeking companies that provide it. For example, a recent survey produced rather startling information: 70% of those polled wanted insurance companies to provide personalized recommendations; help to improve their health and lifestyle; and provide offerings that aligned with their lifestyle and areas of interest.

In light of the study's findings, it would be wise for those providing such services to begin looking at the individual customers' lifestyles and consider how their needs could be best served by the available and future services and how related information can be provided in a clear, understandable, and appealing way.

This approach is vital for the future success of all companies. For example, those involved in wealth management are finding it vital to provide more personalized service than has been available in recent years. True, in years past, little local banks and companies did just that, but as success set in, that approach seemed to fade in many instances. For example, at one time, banks used to offer free checking accounts with no minimum balance requirements and free safety deposit boxes to their customers; that is no longer the case. Instead, banks now charge fees for these items. In addition, banks used to offer personalized services such as a personal banker who helped the bank's clients with advice on investments and other financial matters and provided individualized help when needed. With the rise of online banking, banks have shifted their focus to more digital services and fewer personalized services.

How does the saying go? "Back to the basics." Now, the most successful companies in every industry are investing in building a more personalized approach to providing products, service, and content, and, in order to do so, it is vital that they take a close look at who their customers really are and not depend upon large scale studies of the customer pool in general.

The companies that are the most successful are those that use information as the basis for reconsidering their product lines and service approaches in order to ensure that they more closely fit the needs, interests, and demands of their customers. Such companies are better able to cross-sell and upsell to their customers as well as to plan more effectively for future needs by tailoring their services and approaches accordingly

That takes planning, and that planning has to be based on a sound knowledge base. It is not enough to" cross one's fingers and hope."

Companies must note, consider, and meet shifting demands and thereby be able to provide more customized services and products. AI-powered analytics will make it easier to successfully do just that. The data they will be able to gather in a rapidly changing world will make it possible for them to meet ever-changing customer demands and provide the more personalized service and products that will set them apart from their competitors and lead to greater success.

The most successful companies have always been those that realized that success was dependent upon customer satisfaction, and that is no less true now than it ever was. What has changed is the pace and focus that the present customer base wants and demands. The most successful companies have always been those that were able to provide the information needed and to personalize both it and the related services provided. That hasn't changed, but the speed and format with which both must be delivered has changed, and the companies that strive for great success will take that into consideration and do what successful companies have always done – deliver what their specific customer base wants in the most effective and economical way possible.

In order to accomplish that goal, it is important to build on information that most top companies and individuals already know – only then will humans be able to deliver better one-on-one service when more creativity is required than robots can provide. At the same time, improved self-service or robot-assisted service can also be used, and the effective and balanced use of these approaches will lead to a more satisfied and long-lasting customer-company relationship. By using data already known and by devising an effective process for collecting data from both the known customer and the anonymous pool of customers, companies can be more successful and increase the satisfaction levels of their customers.

AVOIDING REGRET

When a company doesn't meet its customers' expectations, the result is bad customer service and often a loss of revenue. It could be because of what the customer considers is poor quality, poor response time, or a lack of overall satisfaction. Whatever the cause, the result inevitably has a negative impact on customer relations and puts any future business or personal relationships at risk, and that, in turn, has a negative impact upon productivity, success levels, and income.

Let's consider some of the actions (or inactions) that result in what customers may consider "bad service."

One of the actions that is encountered all too often is "putting the customer on hold." According to a survey that was conducted by Voice Response, Inc., two thirds of those surveyed said that they would only be willing to stay on hold for two minutes or less, and thirteen percent said that they were never willing to wait on hold. Most of us have experienced being put on hold, and often the "hold" times are long and may well result in having the connection cut-off. When that occurs, the result is irritation or anger on the part of the person on hold. There are also times when the result goes beyond that, and the person decides to go to a different vendor and, as a result, is lost as a customer or client. In fact, a study done by Velaro found that 60%

of those who were who were put on hold for one minute hung up. It was also found that after about two minutes 34% of the customers who hung up never call back.

The hold time for a phone call varies for a number of reasons – the purpose of the call and the industry being contacted are two major controlling factors. According to a 2012 study conducted by Velaro, 32.3% of the callers indicated that they should never be placed on hold while 27.6% indicated that they would only remain on hold for one to five minutes. The average hold time for a phone call can vary depending on the purpose of the call and the business.

Systems need to be developed, processes used, and staff trained to reduce such hold times and thereby reduce what can be a very costly breach in good customer service and result in the loss of a potentially profitable customer-staff interaction. According to an article on Universal Class, after 30 seconds on hold, many people begin to get irritated. After 60 seconds, 30% of the callers hang up, and if the caller is put on hold for 90 seconds or longer, more than 50% of them hang up. It gets even worse, after two minutes on hold, more than 80% of the customers have already hung up and many of those NEVER call back.

1. One of the things that clients and customers find most irritating is when they encounter multiple transfers prior to reaching the party whom they need to solve a problem or handle a situation. There may be a number of reasons for this problem, but most of them could be fixed by some pre-planning.
   a. Responsibilities can be "tied" to specific titles and operators made aware of this via clearly set forth data.
   b. When the person designated to handle certain kinds of situations or questions is out or away from his/her desk, there needs to be a transfer system in place that puts the inquiring party in touch with a person who can handle the

problem or question right away or at least in a timely manner. The transfer should not take the inquiring party to a voice mail that may or may not ever result in a response. As it is now, there are far too many instances where the caller is put into a very long "wait line", told to call back later, told that someone will call back later, or is just left hanging on the line until he or she runs out of time or gives up in frustration. The ONLY thing that is a sure aftermath to situations like those is irritation which may well cause the customer to go elsewhere in hope that he/she will encounter better customer service. A study by Universal Class showed that after 30 seconds many callers were beginning to feel angry and after 60 seconds 30% had already hung up.

2. There is no question about the importance of a web site and the value it has as a source of information, but when it becomes a means of avoiding providing direct help or answers to a client, it is a detriment rather than an asset to the company. Yet, many companies are using the site as an "answer" location and transferring clients to the site indicating that the solution to whatever it is they need to know is there.

3. Multiple transfers are irritating to clients and may well be the reason a client chooses another vendor or provider. Alternative channels of response need to be devised and USED.

4. Rude behavior, indifference, bad attitudes, and negative or improper language are NEVER acceptable, and may well result in the loss of customers.

5. Although some seem to feel that they are being helpful when they direct the customer or client to the company website, it may not seem that way at all to the inquiring party. That individual may see it as "brush-off" instead.

6. Poorly trained or rude staff members can cost the company a customer or client which, if you'll forgive the pun, could be costly.

7. When a problem doesn't get resolved, it literally becomes a "festering" issue.

The above problems can be readily solved, but there are other problems that may require more effort to ensure that they are handled correctly. For example, companies need to ensure that those dealing with clients directly or indirectly have the knowledge, tools, and information needed to do so effectively and accurately. That requires training, supervision, and it also means that there will also be times when adjustments must be made.

Despite all that, it would be wrong to assume that all break-downs in the service process are due to failures on the part of the staff members. There are times when negative situations are caused by:

1. Angry customers

2. Customers who believe that they are "entitled"

3. Customers who are overly indecisive or cautious

4. So-called penny-pinchers

5. The overly-talkative person

6. The know-it-all customer.

7. The customer who is having a temper tantrum.

Not only do these individuals demand attention, but their approach is also often a barrier to effecttive interaction. Unfortunately, you can't change them, but you do need to develop systems to handle those situations as effectively as possible. Plan ahead and do some joint pre-planning with fellow employees. It always pays to have a plan ready to be used for every situation, particularly the negative ones.

No matter what product you handle, no matter what level of service you provide, regardless of the situation, life will be much easier and the job much more rewarding if you will remember and employ the five keys of good customer service:

PERSONALIZATION

COMPETENCY

CONVENIENCE

PROACTIVITY

PROFESSIONALISM.

THE THREE H'S OF GOOD
CUSTOMER SERVICE

HAPPY CUSTOMERS: Customers who are happy generally become repeat customers, and that translates into the next key factor to success – higher profits.

HIGHER PROFITS: When profits rise, the services to customers can increase, the wages and benefits to employees can increase, and the overall company atmosphere is quite likely to rise as well.

HAPPY EMPLOYEES: Obviously, it is easier to work with colleagues who are happy, and it is easier to keep the customers who feel good about the products and the services provided. Plus, higher profits permit companies to offer higher and more competitive wages that are partially responsible for those feelings.

A key contributing factor to good problem-solving skills is an individual's ability to determine the scope and parameters of a problem and then find the appropriate solution and steps needed to remedy the problem or get to that solution. When those skills are used, the customer's satisfaction is assured, and that goes a long way toward ensuring the success of the company involved.

Another contributing factor to good customer service is patience, which needs to exist in every part of the company. Not all of our customers are outside of the company, some of them are colleagues. There will be situations that trigger the need for every employee to remember that and for each person to endure difficult situations without becoming angry, frustrated, negative, or illogical. Doing so will determine the extent of success in given situations and also the company's success in general.

If they are calm, patient, attentive, and focused, individuals are able to resolve issues more readily, solve problems more effectively, and answer questions more accurately than would otherwise be possible.

There is no doubt that one of the world's most successful men in the 20th Century is Warren Buffet, and it would behoove us all to consider the importance of a statement he once made. "It takes 20 years to develop a reputation and just five minutes to destroy it." The truth of his statement has been proven over and over again as we read the newspapers, listen to newscasts, and learn about the actions of our best-known business people, politicians, and celebrities.

In companies where the employees go above and beyond the expectation levels of their customers and co-workers, the companies are almost always the most lucrative ones in their fields. Two such companies are Zappos and USAA. The opposite is true, however, when a company's sole goal is profit with little, or no, concern about meeting and exceeding the needs of its employees or customers. In those instances, the company's success is doubtful whereas its failure is likely.

The most successful companies are those that know that customer service needs to be multiple-faceted and incorporate service, patience, honesty, respect. quality, efficiency, reliability, sincere interest, concern, and effective aftercare.

Top companies are aware of the importance of customer service and go beyond the minimal level of acceptability and seek to provide for the customers' needs. As part of this process, companies such as Amazon, Hoot Suite, and Tidio use questionnaires--on-line and directly inter-active ones-- to determine how well the needs, interests, and concerns of their clients are being met. According to business.com, some of the big tech companies such as Apple, Verizon, Nest, Lego, and McDonald's conduct surveys to find out what their customers want and then act accord-ingly.

The survey formats differ, but their purpose is the same; however, none of those surveys are of any value if they are only for "show." Far too many of those used by many companies are too cursory and poorly constructed to solicit the input that is really needed in order to ensure that the company can move forward and correct situations that may well need action. There is a definite need to evaluate the customer input and then determine how to best improve in some areas, discontinue some practices, and continue to expand others. According to a Salesforce report, only 68% of customers trust companies to act with society's best interest in mind, and since many customers doubt whether or not anything is ever done as a result of these surveys, it is a good idea for companies to institute a follow-up system that provides information on what was learned and what was done about any problems identified in areas in which customers noted that there was a need to improve. Customers will then be far more likely to provide responses when asked for them.

A good survey is one that provides information regarding the area (e.g., products, services, or experience) under study and/or the group being studied (i.e., customers, employees, target audience, points of concern are some examples). The most successful companies are those that regularly survey their customers and employees and then take action to improve identified weaknesses. When that is done, those surveyed know that the company cares, and the result is generally increased revenues, greater loyalty, higher profits, and, of course, happier clients and staff members who are, in the long run, the greatest advertisements a company can have. Those companies that are successful are those that know this and put into practice the process that brings it about.

Tyson, the largest poultry producer in the U.S., is one example of just such a company. Mattel responded to the public concerns of animal rights activists who are concerned about the treatment of orcas and the safety of trainers, Diet Pepsi stopped using aspartame as a sweetener after consumers protested its use. In other words, there is a great deal of power exerted when the public pressures companies to make changes in their product lines, and wise corporate leaders listen and heed those customers.

CHAPTER 7:
THE ONLY THING
CONSTANT IS CHANGE

Times change, we need to change as well.

Nelson Mandela

Bob Dylan's song, "The Times They Are a-Changin," provides the perfect description of our digital workforce which is automating business and assisting the live agents who at one time played all roles. If anyone asks you if that shift has made a difference in costs, give a resounding, "YES." According to a recent study, service costs have gone up by some 90% while an agent's related time consumption costs are now 15% lower. In addition, the number of calls now handled by live agents has been reduced by an estimated 68%. COST EFFECTIVE – you bet; however, there are some pitfalls in the present system as well.

Many companies depend on automation far too much, and one of the biggest downfalls is their belief that when their telephone lines are busy or when they put people on hold for LONG periods of time that those customers or potential customers will tolerate that. IN MANY CASES THAT IS NOT THE CASE. In 2012, Velaro did a study of some 2,500 customers and found that 60% of them said that they if they had to hold for one minute, they would hang up, 27.6% said they would be willing to hold for one minute, and 32.3% said they were not willing to hold at all. According to <u>Forbes</u>, poor customer service is costing businesses more than $75 billion a year. Callers don't like to be put on hold, tend to hang up, and the result is a negative impact on both the company's profit margin and its reputation. Businesses reported that they lost 75% of the customers who had to wait, and the long waits have a hefty price tag since it is estimated that the cost to retailers is $37 billion in sales each year.

In fact, studies have shown that there is a potential loss of thousands, if not millions, of dollars for those companies. Research done by Valero showed that all it takes is "waiting on hold for one minute for almost 60% of the customers to hang up." Many of those customers will then seek help elsewhere and never come back to the company that in their minds wasted their time. THAT "PLEASE HOLD BUTTON" MAY BE VERY COSTLY!!

The Wharton School in Philadelphia is one of the most advanced business schools in the world, so it is no surprise to find that they have weighed in on the future of the business world. According to Wharton Management Professor, Mauro Guillen, major changes in both the economy and the various aspects of the new technologies will be part of man's future. He went on to say that automation causes technological unemployment.

In his book, <u>2030: How Today's Biggest Trends Will Collide and Reshape the Future of Everything</u>, Dr. Guillen noted that there was the need for mankind to watch "carefully for automation, especially in the service area. We are going to see more automation. We're going to have to think very carefully in political terms and in social terms about the implications of further automation, especially in the service sector."

According to a report prepared by Bain & Company, some 45% of respondents noted that their automation projects had not resulted in the anticipated savings. In part that was because automated equipment requires high capital expenditures since automated systems can cost millions to design, fabricate, and install, and then they require a high level of maintenance. Dr. Guillen is not the only person who is looking at the advances and changes in technology and considering how they will impact man's future and the future of the world in which we live. Consideration must be given to the changes and progress being made in video, real-time messaging, Chatbots, artificial intelligence, cryptocurrencies, and self-service and how they will impact our everyday lives as well as the field of customer service.

Many companies depend on automation far too much, and one of their biggest downfalls is their belief that when their lines are busy or when they put people on hold for LONG periods of time that those customers or potential customers will tolerate that. IN MANY CASES THAT IS NOT THE CASE. In 2012, Velaro did a study of some 2,500 customers and found that 60% of them said that they if they had to hold for one minute, they would hang up, 27.6% said they would be willing to hold for one minute, but 32.3% said they were not willing to hold at all. According to <u>Forbes</u>, poor customer service is costing businesses more than $75 billion a year. Callers don't like to be put on hold, tend to hang up, and the result is a negative impact on both the company's profit margin and its reputation. Businesses reported that they lost 75% of the customers who had to wait, and the long waits have a hefty price tag since it is estimated that the cost to retailers is $37 billion in sales each year.

In fact, studies have shown that there is a potential loss of thousands if not millions of dollars for those companies. Research done by Valero showed that all it takes is "waiting on hold for one minute for almost 60% of the customers to hang up." Many of those customers will then seek help elsewhere and never come back to the company that in their minds wasted their time. THAT "PLEASE HOLD BUTTON" MAY BE VERY COSTLY!!

The Wharton School in Philadelphia is one of the most advanced business schools in the world, so it is no surprise to find that they have weighed in on the future of the business world. According to Wharton Management Professor, Mauro Guillen, major changes in both the economy and the various aspects of the new technologies will be part of man's future. He went on to say that automation will also cause technological unemployment.

In his book, <u>2030: How Today's Biggest Trends Will Collide and Reshape the Future of Everything</u>, Dr. Guillen noted that there was the need for mankind to watch "carefully for automation, especially in the service area. We are going to see more automation. We're going to have to think very carefully in political terms and in social terms about the implications of further automation, especially in the service sector."

According to a report prepared by Bain & Company, some 45% of respondents noted that their automation projects had not resulted in the anticipated savings. In part that was because automated equipment requires high capital expenditures since automated systems can cost millions to design, fabricate, and install, and then it requires a high level of maintenance.

Dr. Guillen is not the only person who is looking at the advances and changes in technology and considering how they will impact man's future and the future of the world in which we live. Consideration must be given to the changes and progress being made in video, real-time messaging, Chatbots, artificial intelligence, crypto-currencies, and self-service and how those changes will impact our everyday lives as well as the field of customer service.

Over the past few years, man has become used to not interacting on a face-to-face basis with his vendors, competitors, and even his associates. But we all know that face-to-face contact facilitates a greater degree of openness than is possible by any other interactive measure. That form of interaction is considered the best business format because it allows for easier persuasion, helps in conflict resolution, helps bring clarity to conversations, saves time, prompts active participation, and helps establish a higher level of trust.

Managers have also noted that when it exists, there is greater job satisfaction, more active participation, and a greater level of trust and productivity. In addition, body language, facial expressions, and nonverbal communication can provide a great deal of information that can result in better communication and more meaningful business relationships. Even so, there is no reason to believe that we will ever go back to our former interaction patterns. The future will probably be a blend of virtual and face-to-face interaction. It is important to realize that collaboration, innovation, acculturation, and dedication are better when there is face-to-face interaction.

Consequently, more and more people are starting to use video voicemail for business, professional, and personal meetings. Those who do so believe that it improves relations and facilitates a degree of openness that is not achieved otherwise. In fact, a number of consultants are encouraging their clients to begin using video voicemail for both personal interaction and group meetings. Video conferencing has become an indispensable daily business tool for many; however, there are some drawbacks to video conferencing. One of the biggest drawbacks is the lack of real-life inter-action. In addition, another disadvantage is the possibility (should we say probability?) of network instability which is a common problem. Add to that the fact that there can be technical issues. That's why many consider hybrid workspace to be the best answer.

Let's consider what actions may be taken and how they may need to change as advances take place.

1. There will be an increasing use of digital media tools making it possible to effectively interact with customers, handle business, and conduct third-party site reviews from separate locations.

2. There is also likely to be a shift to what is known as omni-channel support since it is now possible to sync communication channels together so that both your team and your customers can interact more effectively and work together more readily. One of the reasons for using this approach is that if the situation can't be resolved or the problem solved via this approach, it will be easy to transfer to another medium which can provide better support. That approach is a probable time-saver, and it also makes it possible to move more

quickly toward a solution. Live Chat is truly a vital part of the future.

3. On-site conversations and chat will move into "real time" slots in the near future. That will result in a major change in the effectiveness of man's interaction just as the advent of email created major changes when we were no longer limited to "so-called" snail mail.

4. The changes were, in many instances, tested during the 2023 pandemic. A number of companies shifted employees to the comfort of their own homes while they continued to perform the duties required by their jobs. Were there problems? Of course. Were they all solved? Not at all, but approaches can now be developed that will help systems work more effectively in the future. Now that some of the "kinks" have been worked out, more and more people are comfortable with the idea of working from home. As of 2022, 42% of the U.S. labor force was said to be working from home. As of 2023, 12.7% of the full-time employees worked from home, and 28.2% did so for part of their worktime. That means that 40%+ of the work-force worked remotely, at least in some capacity.

5. Email, live chat, and cloud-based solutions now make it possible to operate from a home base and use the smartphone effectively and, in many cases, more economically than would otherwise be possible. There are some definite drawbacks, however. One of the major ones occurs when the person involved fails to maintain a businesslike approach and allows household chores and personal interactions to lower the professional level of his/her performance.

6. One interesting spin-off of this shift in work location is the fact that it is now affecting multiple professions as well. For example, one psychologist who had previously lived and worked in Chico, California, now lives in Idaho, and is "meeting" with his patients via the internet and telephone. In those instances where physical contact is needed his office staff, which consists of a nurse, receptionist, and a doctor, handles the in-office appointments.

7. Bots (and AI) are helpful, but they are not expected to replace humans. At the present time, most of them are not forms of artificial intelligence but rather just different modes for interaction.

8. One thing that many business owners like about bots is that they provide self-service for customers at the same time that they reduce expenses for vendors. It is no wonder that this new, repeatable, and inexpensive mode of communicating, is growing in popularity.

Our rapidly changing world needs to keep up with bot progress to "stay on the cutting edge of the advances that are going to change many aspects of the business world." One area that will be markedly impacted by the use of the new technology will be the area of customer service which must by its very nature deal with the same issues over and over again. What is now known is that bots can answer multiple questions since they can learn and deliver the same information over and over again.

Well-designed customer service programs provide new strategies, and at some time in the future, bots and AI will play an even greater role in customer service. It is predicted that blockchain technology may well be an integral part of commerce in the not-too-distant future. Social media will probably become a major customer service tool and have a major impact upon service. Many companies are already making use of Facebook and Twitter to make it possible for customers to let their feelings about some business practices be known.

Now a bad customer experience can be recorded and the video uploaded and shared with millions. Since it is estimated that people are likely to trust their peer's opinions, there is a definite need for customer service teams to take note of what is shared on these online sites (e.g., Facebook, You Tube, WhatsApp, Instagram, and WeChat) and have effective response plans ready to put into use. Facebook, Twitter, and Instagram are already a part of the communication channels, and it is now important to view them as customer review channels and realize that they can have a major impact on business success or the lack thereof.

Some companies are already following these sites, making note of the comments made, and taking corrective action as needed. For example, they are using social media monitoring to keep track of keywords, hashtags, and comments relevant to their product/s in order to stay informed about their customers and industry.

It is predicted that in the future more minor customer service problems will be solved by either customer or service technology, and that will make it possible for service representatives to focus on more major problems and thus improve customer service experiences and, hopefully, do so in less time and in a more cost-effective manner than has previously been possible.

SO, YOU HAVE A QUESTION

The more we learn about robotics the more questions we have about how to use them, what problems may result from their use, and how society can benefit from their use. We now know that AI can be used to handle far more than such routine questions as delivery dates, balances owed or paid, the status of an order, due dates, account balances, or other similar questions. It can also be used to enhance the entire customer service process.

Let's consider some of the ways that it can do this.

1. It can be used to lower the end-consumer cost by reducing the cost factor of processing questions and even products.
2. Of course, in our "24-hour" society there is a need for 24-hour service, and AI can provide it at a cost far lower than would be possible than if it were provided only by humans.
3. People hate being put on "hold" and having to wait for help and/or answers to their questions. Such hold time could be markedly reduced since many answers could be provided and needs met by AI.
4. Are these advantages currently available? Not all of them nor are they available in all businesses, but they can be, and probably will be, in the not-too-distant future.

5. By solving 50% or more of the most common questions at the onset, the customer's experiences can be improved, and costs can be reduced.

These service changes are definitely coming, and with them will come needs that in all probability have not yet even been considered. It will, of course, be vital for those in the business community to become familiar with both AI's capabilities and AI's limitations, and it will also be necessary to remember that those capabilities and limitations will undoubtedly change as new uses and problems are identified and solutions designed.

There are a number of steps that can be taken now to help ensure that the move into "the new world" will be effective and that the right "tools" will be available to be used.

1. Define the goals you want to achieve.
2. Identify the problems that you want to solve through the use of AI's applications.
3. Plan ahead and build a team that does the research and takes the needed steps that permit you to select and make use of the tools and technologies that are best suited to your company's needs.
4. Develop an employee training program and make certain that all relevant steps are taken, and all related provisions are in place to ensure that it is implemented.
5. Last, but far from the least, in its level of importance, monitor the results of your implementation process on a continuous basis and make the adjustments that are needed to optimize its success.

Once the pre-steps for AI implementation are all in place, the next step relates to how to best implement an effective contactless customer service program. Many of the approaches that have been used have failed to provide fully satisfactory service insofar as most, or at least many, customers are concerned.

Contactless service is a customer service that is safe, convenient, and satisfactory even though it does not allow for any form of physical contact. The importance of being able to do so was seen in the 2022 worldwide pandemic. There were a number of approaches that were successfully used – Chatbots, virtual assistants, self-service kiosks, mobile apps, and the social media were among those that worked best. Obviously, none of these could be used in instances requiring personal assistance, but they were certainly useful and cost-effective in those instances in which they could be used.

In addition, there are a number of ways in which AI can provide personalized service and thereby ensure availability on a 24-hour basis, reduce costs, and increase efficiency and customer satisfaction. This service can be accomplished by having needs and requests handled quickly now that machine learning can be used to analyze vast quantities of customer interaction data that reveal many of the factors that influence customer attrition such as those noted below.

1. Poor customer service
2. Product or service dissatisfaction
3. Price sensitivity
4. Lack of personalization
5. Inadequate support
6. Long wait times
7. Failure to offer appropriate solutions
8. Misaligned marketing

Let's consider some of the ways that with AI's help customers receive more personalized learning experiences:

1. 24/7 availability can be provided.
2. Costs can be reduced.
3. Efficiency can be improved.
4. Customer engagement can be improved.

Studies have shown that the companies that employ AI tend to have a client retention rate some 3.3 times higher than those companies that do not do so. Why is this? The companies that use machine learning are able to have vast volumes of data related to customer interaction studied and analyzed, and they able to identify the factors that influence customer turnover. If the data is used properly, they can develop the effective measures needed to solve problems. According to a 2020 Deloitte survey, 67% of companies are now using machine learning and 97% plan to use it in the near future. Amazon Web Service, Veritone, DataRobot, SoundHound, and Unity-Interactions are among those using it.

It is not surprising that there is interest in knowing how to acquire such information quickly and make sure that it is highly accurate since being able to do so places a company in a far better position than their competitors. Why? Because the company is then able to resolve issues and maintain service levels that are more satisfactory and less costly than would otherwise be possible.

Of course, there are some disadvantages to this approach, so let's take a look at those, too.

1. There is definitely a higher initial cost.
2. There is a dependence on data quality and data availability, and nothing is perfect, man or machine. There could be errors and those errors could result in actions that might well create problems.
3. It is difficult to integrate the presently used systems and AI.
4. There are a number of ethical and legal concerns about data privacy and security that need to be considered and handled.

New laws are being drafted in both Europe and the U.S. that make it illegal to use personal data secured via AI systems. It is known that people need to be careful about what they share when prompted by Chatbots or any other AI tools. For example, a lawyer's citation of court decisions fabricated by ChatGPT shows the danger of relying on such information without proper safeguards. In fact, in Italy, ChatGPT has been banned from even operating after the "country's data protection regulator said that there was no legal basis to justify the collection of 'massive storage' of personal data.

The National Conference of State Legislatures has compiled a list of legislations related to artificial intelligence issues, and Washington provided the funding for the Chief Information Officer to convene a work-related group to examine how automated decision-making systems can be reviewed and periodically audited. There are also questions related to copyright laws that need answers. Those questions relate to authorship, infringement, and the fair use of content created or used by AI.

There are already hundreds of data brokers gathering personal data. At the present time, the only sure way to protect oneself is to keep personal data off the net – don't share it and remove what has already been shared. There have been recent news items related to this topic, and the problems that have been identified are numerous.

Because of the dangers involved, there are increased concerns, and some suggestions have been made regarding ways that one can protect oneself. Those suggestions are shown below:

1. Use strong passwords and change them regularly.
2. Be careful about the personal information you share online.
3. Use two-factor authentication whenever possible.
4. Keep your software up-to-date.
5. Use a VPN (virtual private network) when browsing the net.
6. Be cautious about phishing scams.
7. Limit the amount of personal information you share on social media.

Even though there are still many questions unanswered, a number of problems still unsolved, and issues that still need to be resolved, it is believed that AI users "enjoy 3.5 times greater annual improvement in customer satisfaction rates than do their competitors and eight times greater annual improvement rate in customer effort scores." Therefore, it is not at all surprising to learn that it is estimated that more than 90% of the companies selling top brands and having a high level of customer satisfaction are already using AI solutions to handle customer concerns as a means of increasing satisfaction. As more and more companies are choosing to use AI, it is becoming an integral part of conducting business and provides numerous benefits and opportunities for growth and will certainly revolutionize the way business is done.

This is particularly true in the area of customer service because the AI systems can "understand" numerous languages, analyze customer data, and personalize the responses to questions. People are very positive about their experiences with companies that use this new technology. They like the fact that their routine questions and requests get quick and accurate responses, and both companies and their customers are profiting from the time saved.

Besides, those companies that are using AI as a basis for data analysis are finding it easier to handle the process than it was in the past. There has been an unbelievable growth of data in the past few years, and AI algorithms are able to process larger volumes of data and do so more quickly than humans can or ever could have.

Managers can now make more informed decisions than they could before.

By using AI, companies have been able to become more competitive and better able to make data-based decisions and thereby identify business opportunities and problems that might have been overlooked in the past. There has also been a positive impact upon the marketing and advertising programs of those companies that have used AI as the base for their analysis of everything from customer preferences and be-haviors to customer-based demographics. The resultant data has allowed them to better understand their target market and personalize their advertisements and their recommendations.

How? Well, AI-powered recommendations are based on previous purchases, choices, and browsing history, and that data makes it possible to make valid predictions about the areas of interest which are the basis for a client's eventual choices and decisions.

AI's use is revolutionizing many companies including those in the healthcare industry where it is making major changes in medical research, diagnosis, patient treatment, and staff burnout. With AI algorithms, it is now possible to analyze vast amounts of data, review patients' records, staff attendance, and employment records, and make correlations between the information stored and the actions proposed. Accurate and timely action makes it possible to detect and handle issues at an early stage thereby avoiding major problems.

The use of AI goes beyond the medical field, and its importance to the manufacturing sector is well-known. It is being used to improve efficiency and productivity by automating the production pro-cess. It is also used to monitor equipment perform-ance and predict maintenance needs.

The result in reduced downtime, improved production, and overall operational efficiency has reduced costs and, hopefully, that reduction will be passed along to the consumer, too.

Other industries are also benefiting from the capabilities of AI. For example, in the financial field, AI has made it possible to improve the process of fraud detection thus reducing risks and improving investment management techniques. Risk management models powered by AI are helping financial institutions evaluate credit-worthiness and thereby make better lending decisions and identify better investment opportunities.

AI has become the guru of the financial world and is being used in multiple ways: customer service, data analysis, marketing, healthcare, supply chain management, finance, and also for investment management. There is no doubt that the world of finance is not the same as it once was, and these changes have been noted in financial publications such as <u>Forbes</u>, the <u>Harvard Business Review</u>, and the <u>MIT Technology Review</u>.

The financial industry has been transformed, and the digital payment system is a revolution in an industry which never expected to have to deal with the changes that have occurred. In addition to being able to handle many transactions over a mobile phone, there is now the alternative of using digital currencies in lieu of traditional currencies. Mobile banking and payments are increasing, and fewer people are actually visiting bank branches while new software programs are streamlining work for both businesses and individuals.

Automation technologies and machine learning are going to play a major role in all aspects of our culture and will become the focus of a great deal of public attention and concern. In fact, they have already triggered a guessing game – Will my job become extinct? What jobs will still exist? Will our services even be needed? There is a good reason for those questions to be asked because there will definitely be changes and transformations in many fields particularly those that require a great deal of "knowledge work."

There is a likelihood that automation will result in the elimination of many jobs in the next ten years, and it will also impact most jobs in most fields to some degree. There will be a literal transformation in the way many jobs in the healthcare and finance industries are performed, and that transformation is already occurring. Overall, the percentage of jobs that have already been negatively impacted by automaton is of great concern. One citation noted that 47% of jobs will be susceptible to automation before 2030, and jobs requiring a lower level of education and jobs that require the performance of routine tasks are those most likely to be subject to automation. Researchers estimate that somewhere between 9% to 47% of jobs could be automated in the future.

In fact, according to the Organization for Economic Cooperation and Development, it is only a matter of time before the negative impact upon employment will be significant. It was noted that over twenty-five percent of the jobs in OECD countries involved tasks that AI could perform, e.g., customer service, research, accounting, paralegal, and radiology to name just a few. Note that this list includes both trained and blue-collar jobs. Robot waiters are already on the job in one Colorado restaurant, and Bella Italia in England, Sergio's Restaurant in Oaklahoma, and Robotazia in England all use robots in lieu of waiters.

According to Reuters, the jobs that are most likely to be negatively impacted are those which require more than 25 of the 100 skills that AI has.

According to a report from Oxford Economics, about 8.5% of the global workforce could be displaced by robots by the year 2030. That means that robots and automation could result in the displacement of 20 million manufacturing jobs by that year. Some of the most in-demand skills for AI include critical thinking, problem solving, an eye for detail, curiosity, and creativity.

In fact, the OECD (Organization for Economic Cooperation and Development) said that it is only a matter of time before the impact is negative. Will it be worth the cost? That is not yet known.

That the use of AI will impact the business world is a given, for there are many jobs that AI can do (e.g., those that do not require high levels of either social or emotional intelligence); however, there are many reasons why certain positions are very unlikely to ever be filled by robots because robots lack emotional intelligence, can't function without input, and need to be fact-checked. The jobs that AI can do are those jobs that can be readily automated, involve little or no interaction with people, and do not require a high level of social or emotional intelligence. It will be those jobs that are most likely to be heavily impacted by the use of AI.

There are some people who believe that the impact AI will go far beyond the level presently predicted and point to a recent "interview" of a robot that was posted on the net and was fascinating reading. That interview was conducted by Blake Lemoine and was with the robot that he stated had become sentient. As result of his contention, Lemoine was dismissed from his job at Google on the basis that he had violated their policies that related to the secrecy of their research projects.

CHAPTER 8:
COULD MACHINES REPLACE HUMANS?

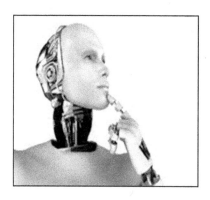

The rapid changing and reshaping of the world that has always been is creating both fear and excitement. Some are asking if humans can be replaced by machines, and those fears are being expressed in many ways. In fact, in my recently published book entitled, <u>A Look at The Unexplained,</u> I noted that robots have been designed that can not only perform given tasks but are also able to interact, communicate, and think at very advanced levels. It was reported that one such robot, Sophia, is "without a doubt a fascinating creation" and "could be man's undoing." This very humanlike creation is able to function in a near-human manner, form opinions, think, and appar-

ently, she can also set goals for herself as well. In one interactive session, she told her creator, Dr. David Hanson (the founder of Hanson Robotics), that she would "destroy humans."

In light of "her" comment, it is interesting that McKinsey now estimates that AI will "reach the top quartile of human ability in creativity, natural language generation, and understanding of social and emotional reasoning and sensing an astonishing 20 to 25 years earlier than was previously estimated in 2017."

In addition, he predicted that by 2030, AI will have reached a stage of development in logical reasoning, problem solving, articulation, presentations, sensory perception, and both social and emotional output where she" will be better than three-quarters of the human workers." If he is right, AI will transform and even automate jobs in the near future – jobs that might otherwise have taken decades to automate.

The question that then comes to mind is, "Will this really happen? Will it mean that humans are eclipsed or replaced by machines?" Every time I consider those questions, I remember a play by Capek, <u>R.U.R.-- Rosums Universal Robots</u>, and am amazed by the fact that so little of what he shared in that play was ever considered to be a possible preview of man's future, and yet he was amazingly accurate in his "predictions."

Brent Orrell, a senior fellow at the American Enterprise Institute, suggests that we look at present and potential situations another way. Are soft skills shortages partially responsible for many of our problems today – social conflict and poverty and their multiple ramifications? Could these advances actually be the solution needed to close our soft-skills gap? It could be! In fact, there was a study conducted at Stanford University that found that the use of the new technology "raised job performance among lower-skilled customer service representatives by helping them better manage social interactions" with frustrated callers. This may well be the technology needed to make it possible for those lacking in those needed skills to function far more effectively and thereby benefit both themselves and the workplace.

The impact of artificial intelligence is now revolutionizing the business world, and many companies can now, with the help of AI, operate in ways that will transform some operating procedures, eliminate some, and initiate others previously unknown. When it is considered that this change can apply to some 53% of the business world's activities that we are told can be automated, the impact and its consequences must be considered carefully.

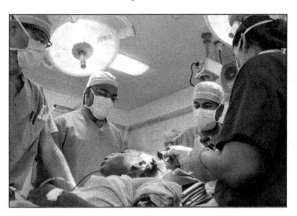

One of the industries that may see the most change is the healthcare industry where AI can help in the diagnosis of diseases, analyze medical images, predict the outcome of given treatments, enhance diagnostic accuracy, and improve the ordering and allocation of medical supplies. Of equal, if not greater importance, is the fact that AI can even make accurate diagnoses of medical problems and perform minor (at least for now only minor) surgeries efficiently and precisely. Of course, that brings up a question that must be considered – how would people feel about having AI perform their surgery?

These medical advances will make it possible to improve patient care as well as medical diagnostic accuracy and may even have a very positive impact upon both medical resource allocation and the accuracy of medical diagnoses.

Medicine is not the only field that will be impacted by these advances, the finance industry is a sector that will also experience major changes and disruptions as well. Routine tasks such as fraud detection, credit score checks, and simple orders will be increasingly handled by AI as a means of increasing efficiency and reducing costs. For many of the same reasons, the manufacturing industry will turn to AI-powered robots as a way of streamlining production by enhancing quality control measures and increasing productivity. All of these changes will make it possible to not only increase productivity but to also reduce costs and improve quality at the same time.

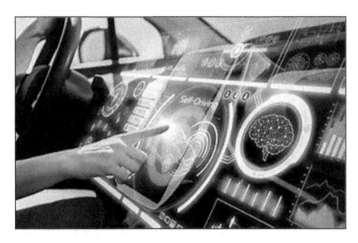

The transportation industry will undergo some of the most significant changes when self-driving vehicles powered by AI algorithms are used on an increased basis. It is believed that their use will revolutionize our entire transportation system, reduce road congestion, and even have a positive impact on fuel consumption and road safety.

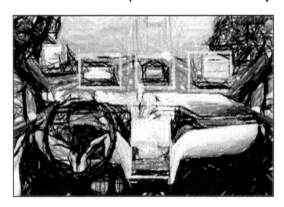

In 2019, there were more than 1,400 self-driving cars, trucks, and other vehicles being tested by more than 80 companies in the United States.

Through the utilization of the new systems, it is expected that there will be better planning, predicting, and demand patterns, and, if the estimations are right, there should also be a reduction in cost and an increase in overall safety. This projection extends to many industries, and a greater level of personalized service and planning is expected to come into being thus providing better support and enhancing every aspect of purchasing and planning after the initial stages which may well be very costly.

Because the use of new technology will permit data to be more readily available and more accurately used to predict buying patterns and demands, it will be possible to automate more aspects of the "buying process" and thereby make the entire operational process more efficient than it is now. It is predicted that the result of those changes will be an increase in sales, better management of inventories, and, of course, a better level of service as far as the customers are concerned.

Through an increased use of AI, it is believed that almost every facet of our modern world can be improved, even the field of education. AI can be used to personalize and individualize the educational process by tailoring learning and feedback to each individual student's needs, and it can do so via automated grading and feedback. Of course, all of these changes require a total revamping of the educational training programs designed for educators. This also means there is a need to revamp our educational institutions and retrain the present educational staff. That will not be an easy process, it will require major changes at the undergraduate and graduate levels, and there may well be reluctance on the part of those educators who must be retrained in order to make it possible to initiate the needed changes. It will also be a costly process and funding will undoubtedly require increased taxation. All of these factors must be carefully considered, and appropriate plans put into place so that the changes can occur. This won't be easy, and there may well be a great deal of resistance to the needed changes.

Vast amounts of data can be analyzed and used to help in the selection and development of the most effective teaching methods and the best tools, and the result is expected to lead to a major improvement in both teaching strategies and learning outcomes.

Of course, changes will occur in every field, even agriculture where AI-powered drones can be used to monitor crops, optimize practices in general, and detect minor problems so that they can be addressed before they become major ones. For the first time in the history of man, accurate predictions can be made through the analyzation of the data related to all aspects of the agricultural process thus making it possible to automate tasks in every area of agriculture thereby improving efficiency while increasing yield and reducing waste.

The scope of the changes that can occur goes beyond present demands, and the ways in which the use of AI will be able to improve the management of energy storage, the accuracy of predictions, and the prevention of breakdowns and problems is beyond our current level of understanding.

Literally every facet of our world will be impacted by AI and its related technologies because it can analyze given situations and then provide related recommendations. In fact, even the entertainment industry will be able to profit from the use of this new technology – scripts and music can be developed, and all content can be personalized, streamlined, and more consistently delivered. Of course, there are negatives as well, and as is already happening in the field of literature, technologically created productions will come into existence, too.

As far apart as are the entertainment and legal industries, one might question whether both could profit from this new technology, but there is no doubt that they will be impacted by it. AI can provide both fields with research assistance, relevant insights, contract analysis, and document review all of which will increase efficiency, reduce costs, and improve the accuracy in both.

In other words, according to the reports provided by sources such as <u>Forbes</u> and McKinsey and Company, AI is expected to make major changes to and have a significant impact upon multiple industries, and, if this is so, then the world as we have always known it will be far different from the world that is to come.

DON'T FORGET ONE OF SOCIETY'S MOST IMPORTANT FIELDS--EDUCATION

The impact of education on almost every endeavor and every aspect of life is often ignored, and yet it provides the foundation upon which all else builds, so let's take a closer look at the ways in which AI is likely to change, and even revolutionize, the existing educational system as well as the teaching methods and learning experiences.

The use of AI will undoubtedly make major changes in what we have always known as our educational system. Learning experiences can be made more personal, teaching methods will be markedly modified, and valuable insights into student performance can be made available. In essence, the use of AI-related technologies will provide educators with the tools needed to markedly alter the learning environment, but those tools will also pose challenges and ethical questions that will need to be addressed.

Let's look at those and consider them in more detail. TV has been increasingly used as an educational tool, and now it is likely that it will continue to be used with the added aid of Chatbots. In fact, there is a British program whose host posed complex questions which were then answered in a most interesting way by a Chatbot.

The Three C's

One of the positive changes that AI can provide is an educational system that allows a more personalized approach to learning since it will be possible to provide teachers with analyzed data on individual students – their strengths, weaknesses, interests, and learning styles are all areas that could be analyzed and the results provided making it easier for teachers to tailor assignments and approaches to the individual child. The operative word here is "could," but in order to utilize the newly available tools, there is a need to develop ways to make sure that they are provided and that teachers are trained to utilize the information effectively.

Teachers will also be able to provide instruction at the pace best suited to a given child's specific needs. It is known that students learn best when they can do so at their own pace and from approaches that are keyed to their individual learning styles. Of course, that means that the educational programs provided to teachers must take that into consideration and tailor the educational offerings so that they provide the needed approaches and resources to implement such an approach. When teachers design, implement, and teach in ways that are tailored to the individual learning styles of their students, there is a definite and noticeable improvement in the academic outcomes.

The effectiveness of any educational program goes beyond the classroom presentation styles of the teachers. There is also a need to be able to effectively handle the administrative demands such as grading papers, managing records, and scheduling classes and related program offerings. All of these demands can be made easier and less burdensome by using AI-powered systems thus allowing the teachers more time to do what is the most important part of the educational process – providing the individualized attention and feedback necessary for educational success.

In addition, AI can be used to provide individualized coaching and tutoring programs by simulating one-on-one interactions with tutors and thereby helping students grasp difficult concepts more readily. AI can also be used to analyze student feedback and simulate one-on-one interactions on a 24/7 basis if that is wanted, and it can be used to provide effective guidance as well.

The fact that virtual reality can augment actual reality makes it possible to create realistic simulations that can be used to help students better understand what might otherwise be too complex for many of them to grasp. For example, history students can gain a better understanding of historical events through what is known as "immersive" AR experiences which use digital technology to imitate or create a real or imagined world that surrounds the users and lets them literally interact with it. The purpose is to evoke a sense of immersion and emotion, and thereby enhance the learning experience. Because the learner is fully immersed in the subject matter, this is a very effective learning experience since it allows the learner to fully engage with the material and learn through experience.

The Walton Family Foundation did a study of one school district and found that 40 percent of those surveyed said that they used CHATGPT at least once a week, and 53 percent anticipated increased use.

One of the teachers had asked ChatGPT to generate ten different project options for her sci-fi unit. Instead of a traditional essay assignment, the program suggested imaginative projects such as creating and explaining a poster to an alien.

The ChatGPT can also translate assignments to a student's native language and thereby make it easier for the student to comply with a request.

One of the major concerns is the fact that students have been found to use the chatbot to cheat, and many educators have noted that, and they are now spending time checking for AI plagiarism and revamping their lesson plans to make them "AI-proof". Until the risks to academic integrity can be handled effectively, a number of school districts have chosen to ban ChatGPT.

The center for Teaching Innovation at Cornell University provides information on ways to identify and address student learning gaps. AI can identify learning gaps thereby making it possible to accomplish what has not been possible before – recognize patterns and trends that indicate the areas that are problems for given students. AI can also make related information available to instructors that was never available before and thereby make it possible for the instructor to target problem areas at a far earlier stage than would have otherwise been possible.

Also, by having access to that information, educators can design effective teaching strategies, create appropriate curriculum offerings, and consider more effective ways to integrate AI into their teaching strategies. Of course, all of this means that the training programs for teachers will need to be modified and provide the tools and foundations needed to effectively employ such strategies. In essence, there is going to have to be a major overhaul of educational programs provided to would-be educators and those who are already in the educational field but who have never been introduced to the programs that will need to be implemented.

According to EdSource, mid-career teacher training should focus on academic subjects, content, active learning, collaboration, coaching, and subject content. Global Partnership for Education recommends that educators need deep content knowledge, and the ability to implement different models of instructional strategies, assessment practices, and assessment methods.

It is also true that all of these new strategies might create ethical concerns which will have to be handled. The information that can be utilized must be used responsibly and individual privacy protected because there are definitely ethical considerations that must be addressed.

The EdExec Summit is a new event from Tech and Learning that is designed to bring together for three days executives from those companies that serve the educational community, and during that time, the focus will be on three specific areas that educators consider to be important if there is to be an effective use of AI in educational offerings.

- Personalization
- Support for educators
- Enhanced interaction.

It is projected that teaching and learning processes will be impacted in a number of ways when AI is used:

1. Increased efficiency
2. Better feedback to students
3. Greater level of customization
4. Earlier intervention if needed

5. Better targeted support
6. More engaging and interactive programs.
7. A wider variety of resources and more personalized materials and feedback.

Educators have mixed feelings about the use of this new tool, but, even so, many teachers are already using it to help develop teaching strategies and create emails and tests. The use of this tool has been forbidden in some school districts like N.Y.C and L.A.U.S.D. because the directors in those districts have real concerns about how their use will impact learning and the degree to which cheating will increase. The fact that this technology makes mistakes, invents facts, and may well contain errors has prompted many educators to move cautiously.

There are concerns about how AI tools might harm the educational system. There is a fear that they might be used to replace human teachers and thus cost jobs, and it is also feared that AI tools could be biased and perpetuate the already existing inequalities in the educational system. In addition, there are concerns about data privacy and security, but it is believed that AI can help in many ways as well (e.g., provide targeted intervention for students in need of extra help, and automate grading and feedback procedures) as long as steps are taken to ensure that AI is used ethically and responsibly.

Information and tips regarding the use and potential problems are being sought; and there are now more than 250,000 people who have signed onto one of the most popular pages on Facebook (ChatGPT for Teachers). There are many who believe that the idea of making use of this tool is a good one, but there is also a need for caution and a step-by-step evaluation process needs to be put into place before any major changes take place. If that isn't done, AI could actually do a great deal of harm to our educational process.

If AI is only used to provide assistance, then it is a truly valuable tool, but if students use it to cheat, they will lose a great deal. The human touch is still needed, but there is no doubt that the bots can have an important place in our educational programs.

Dr. Stuart Geiger, a professor at the University of California at San Diego, requires his students to write "a reflective passage alongside each of their assignments about the writing process." They are asked to document what sources they're using and how a site such as Google Scholar or a certain database might skew their results.

Dr. Geiger points out that ChatGPT is able to answer every question posed but that doesn't mean that the answers are correct. But since it sounds so authoritative, it is likely that many will accept those answers and assume that they are accurate. We all need to realize that the easy way may well be the wrong way. According to a study done by New Scientist, AI search engines often fail to back up their statements or cite incorrect information even though the answers may sound convincing. Microsoft noted that although AI does have a tendency to give wrong answers, they are "usefully wrong."

OpenAI can be used to generate unique problem sets and reading materials that are tailored to each student's needs, and it can also be used to detect problems such as learning disabilities. At a conference held in 2023, Adam Garry, Senior Director of Education Strategy at Dell, discussed the future of K-12 technical education as it involved generative AI. "Since the pandemic, we have shifted the nature of how technology is used in the schools. Future Source Data shows that

98% of the school districts have a one-to-one system for their students. Generative AI could generate unique problem sets or reading materials adapted to each student's skill level," Garry said. "It could also be used to simulate realistic virtual experiences or make topics more relatable and engaging."

He went on to note that AI would also be able to help in the detection of learning disabilities, provide timely interventions, or even provide the assistance needed that would give teachers more time to focus on individual students. He pointed out that Dell Technologies helps their district partners across North America by providing eight free learning modules designed to explore the opportunities and challenges of using AI. He went on to suggest that schools focus on identifying misinformation and building the skills needed with new digital literacies. "Generative AI will likely revolutionize teaching and learning...we could see more personalized learning experiences where AI tailors the curriculum to the individual student's strengths, weaknesses, and pace."

"We need to ensure that the use of AI is transparent, secure, and respects privacy," said Garry. "School districts should draft memos to companies when products have been updated with generative AI and ask what data sources are informing the model was used and where data being gathered will go and how it will be used."

It is definite that AI is making significant changes in the entire educational process, and, if properly implemented, the results should be positive ones and the students impacted should literally learn more quickly and be able to advance faster resulting in a world that moves smoothly into a future that will be markedly different from the world we know.

CHAPTER 9:
WHAT ROLE CAN AI PLAY IN IMPROVING CUSTOMER SERVICE?

Artificial intelligence (AI) makes it possible for companies to identify the "pluses and minuses of their delivery of customer service in real time." Since service is not something that can be designed to "fit everyone every time", it is vital for companies to utilize all of the tools at their disposal to identify what their customer's (and in some instances their staff's which form part of that customer pool) needs are, review those needs, and then evaluate what assistance can be provided and how to best provide it.

In light of what is known as "expectation transfer" which occurs when companies find themselves in the position of NEEDING to raise the bar on their products and delivery process in order to remain in a competitive position in their industry, related studies are vital. Andy Traba, the head of product marketing for the Analytics Division of NICE, stated it very clearly when he said, "Expectation transfer occurs when one key business raises the bar, and consumers then expect that across the board."

It has long been known that success comes to those who know, recognize. and act in accord with the concept that service is not a "one-size-fits-all" proposition. The use of AI permits companies to instantly analyze data and then quickly make the needed adjustments in order to alter and differentiate the service they provide.

Success is based on these key factors: personalization, convenience, and interaction that is hassle-free, but since there is no one-size-fits-all formula for service, it is vital that the people involved and the "machines" that support them make the right decisions at the right times, respond appropriately in what are often unique situations, and address the identified customer's needs.

Just as the first moon landing changed the history of space study when in January of 1966 NASA sent up the first unmanned Apollo, Customer Service AI has made it possible for those in business to use an efficient and effective mode of analysis to analyze and elevate every facet of customer service. By tracking conversations, monitoring speech patterns and language usage, and generating psychographic profiles, AI is able to make logical and valid predictions about future needs, reactions, and purchase or rejection patterns.

AI can even match consumers to providers based on unique needs, and "can extend this capability to predict emotion and intent, make the perfect match, and discover the best opportunity for automation." This can extend to the delivery stage, even for those customers who do not interact directly with a customer service agent.

One of the most interesting aspects of customer service automation is the attitude of those who are using it. The following comments make their position clear.

> According to Craig Vincent who is the head of Global Success Programs, "We've seen our engagement rates rise by 25–30%, product activation has increased by 11% across the board, and [Intercom's] automation capabilities have helped us to scale our efforts without increasing headcount, which has saved us $1 million."

> Brian Lederman, the Head of Sales, Support, and Success at Coda, had this to say, "Since we introduced Custom Bots, our Support team has been able to save time and reduce their median reply count for certain queries by 57% – from seven replies to just three."

> Geronimo Chala, the Chief Consumer Officer at Rebag, put it another way, "The happier our team is, the easier it is for them to delight our customers. So, Intercom was that one position that tied all of those pieces together for us. We fell in love with it."

When you realize that the use of customer service automation can resolve issues faster and boost satisfaction levels higher at the same time that there is a reduction of the number of demands placed on teams, you can understand why comments such as those are being heard throughout the various industries that employ customer service automation.

Those companies using AI supported customer service do so because they believe that it helps them better understand their customers' needs and responses and thereby makes it possible for them to improve and, in turn, produces positive outcomes in the following areas:

1. Customer satisfaction,
2. Employee retention rates,

3. Brand recognition and satisfaction,
4. Planning processes,
5. Revenue increases,
6. Preventative approaches.

When positive outcomes are added to the new solutions that AI can provide, a whole new perspective of customer service comes into view. It is important to remember that some 96% of consumers are heavily influenced by the level of customer service provided to them, and, in many instances, their reactions play an important role in their decision to continue (or discontinue) using the services or products of a particular company. Artificial intelligence is the key to enabling real-time service for customer support platforms, and what's more, this technology has the potential to change the way customer service solutions are developed.

It is now possible to literally "teach" and "train" a machine by using NLP (natural language processing) which is a subset of what is called Machine Learning and its subset, NLP, or natural language processing. Machine learning makes it possible for machines to perform without having been specifically programmed to take given actions. Instead, they can "act appropriately by utilizing patterns that are based on earlier data."

In addition, AI can process vast amounts of data and do so quickly and accurately once the format and rules have been established. The process is simplified by the use of NLP (natural language processing) which enables machines to understand both spoken and written messages and then provide an appropriate response.

By using data analytics, data can easily be examined and organized. Obviously, although this is readily done with structured data, unstructured data such as audio, video, photos, open-ended questions, and online reviews makes such examination far more difficult. In between these two extremes is semi-structured data. The successful use of AI will only be as good as the data fed it. So, let's take a closer look at the process.

Many companies are now using Chatbots to answer basic questions about such things as delivery dates, account balances, order status, and even potential alternatives to the items selected or ordered. When this is done, the staff is left free to deal with more complex problems and issues, and thus operating costs are generally lowered.

In an increasingly international business world, the fact that AI can be programmed to "converse" in several languages can be a major asset insofar as both the company and customers are concerned. Multilingual customer care can be a major factor in attracting and serving an international customer base.

It is important to remember, however, that AI is still a machine, and its function is only as successful as the data fed it. Nevertheless, AI can be used as an excellent customer service tool, so let's consider how that can be done and the benefits it can produce.

1. Support can be speeded up markedly and instant replies provided.
2. Solutions can be provided at a much quicker rate than would otherwise be possible.
3. Problem-solving tends to be much faster and improves customer satisfaction levels.
4. There can be greater consistency.
5. Problems and issues can be handled on a 24-hour basis.
6. There can be a reduction in human error and the negative consequences therefrom

We all make mistakes—but AI-based models are trained to be accurate and precise. The more data they process, the more accurate they become. This means that the more you use it, the better the results. However, AI depends on available data, and the output may well be negatively impacted if new data is not available or if the data that is available is inaccurate.

The use of automated customer service can help you to identify possible leads, trace market flow, and help you plan your marketing by analyzing leads and identifying the market. The fact that you can now collect data quickly means that you are able to take actions that can improve customer service and product delivery.

For example, with the use of automated text analysis, it is possible to spot repetitions and possible problems. That analysis also makes it possible to notice trends and make the needed changes and adjustments and thereby eliminate problems, improve delivery, and increase the level of satisfaction. Customers are happier when you provide speedy support, and happy customers are always a company's best form of advertising.

Those in the industry talk about "training your data" -- a process that involves uploading data—text or images—to predetermined labels. That *'training data,'* is basically what AI learns from. There are four steps that are vital.

1. To ensure success
2. To determine what's wanted
3. To identify what's needed
4. To design the steps to take, and how to implement those steps,

Once those steps have been taken, you are on the road to success. The next steps that need to be taken are normalization, conversion, missing value imputation, and resampling.

Now, let's consider what else needs to be done to show that you really do believe that "the customer always comes first." The basis of success hasn't really changed over the years – companies that know their customers and cater to their needs and lifestyles are the companies that succeed and become the role models that others strive to emulate.

If you learn what customers need and then do what is needed to provide the right support and service, AI's efforts can be leveraged to improve customer service and thereby increase the success of a company. A major key to corporate success is its ability to duplicate the practices that have been proven to work. Here are some of the successful practices and methods that have been identified by Forbes Business Council members.

1. Solve Users' Most Frequent Questions

"We have extensively used AI chatbots for ourselves and our clients to solve the most frequently asked questions raised by users. By solving over 50% of recurring questions from the outset, we are able to significantly improve the user experience while simultaneously cutting costs for the organization." - Nate Nead, DEV.co

2. Learn Customer Behavior Patterns

"Build intelligent customized experiences. AI can be used to learn patterns of customer behavior (like purchasing cycles on a credit card, retail spending or travel) and then forecast behavior accordingly. Then when the customer contacts the organization, these patterns can be used to offer the most likely service options or information based on the time and date of previous activities. "- Janine Bensouda, Bensouda Consulting

3. Speed Up Response Times

"As an AI company as well, we see a lot of value in the customer service use case. I'm an advisor to a SaaS company that leverages AI to speed up the response time of customer support agents. They use AI to clearly identify the needs of the customer and display the right information to the agents, thus bringing best-in-class customer service. Forethought in SF is also great." – Gaspard deLacroix, Skypher

4. Utilize Natural Language To Increase Understanding

"Organizations can leverage AI by utilizing natural language understanding (NLU). By using real-time analysis of customer service calls, chats, and emails, they can understand the conversation between the customer service representative and the customer. AI can offer ways to improve the customer experience via understanding the customer's level of frustration, the need for escalation and quicker resolution of problems." - Oded Agam, Next Leap Ventures

5. Anticipate Trends, Sentiment, Events

The massive volumes of public data produced globally each second allow for AI-enabled predictive anticipation of trends, sentiment, and key events of interest. This unlocks powerful new possibilities to anticipate and address issues in various markets while proactively mitigating malicious digital threats to your business, brand, or customers— a critical but under-emphasized element of CX.- Alejandro Romero, Constella Intelligence

6. Enhance Human Interaction

The best utilization of AI is not to replace human interaction, but to enhance human interaction and decrease the friction in the customer experience. As an example, if there are tech questions such as resetting passwords that can be directed through AI responses, that is a great use of the resource. However, businesses need to be careful not to underwhelm the customer by removing the human touch. - Veena Jetti, Vive Funds

7. Measure Customer Wait Times

AI can now let you measure customer wait times. This is particularly important in the service industry, restaurants for example, where time in line (or drive-thru) has a huge revenue impact. Historically, poor service has been difficult to track. With computer vision AI, you can collect actionable insights on each interaction and use that transparency to perfect your customer service.- Alex Popper, Hello-meter

8. Capture Large Amounts of Data

Organizations must be specific about who AI "serves." In healthcare, human interaction is critical to providing patient care, while AI is best suited to serve physicians. For example, a common complaint is the amount of data required to meet quality metrics and risk coding. AI can capture data with its mining and recognition capabilities from workflows allowing physicians time for patient care. - Vijay Murugappan, First Quadrant Advisory

9. Suggest Actions for Agents

Agents can be more effective in customer interactions with the help of AI. A tech firm built a recommendation system using ticket and remediation history, interactions, etc., that proactively suggests the next actions for agents. With this solution that had a data lake for different types of data, multiple NLP pipelines and a business graph, NPS ratings improved and time to resolution was reduced --Analytics Solutions

10. Embrace Speech Analytics

One of the most interesting paths to leveraging AI in customer service is speech analytics. It's a very hot space with major cloud players (Microsoft, AWS, Google) investing. Speech analytics gives management insight into which calls are the most effective, which CSRs are the best, and what training and operational changes can make customer service more successful. - Sandeep Bhargava,

11. Personalize

AI can personalize communication, and then organizations can implement AI-generated content into communication with clients. Would you like to receive assistance from support with the voice of Homer Simpson? (**Homer Jay Simpson** is a fictional character and the main protagonist of the American animated sitcom *The Simpsons*.) AI can manage it in a second. It can be a winning strategy for businesses competing in a creative niche. One more example is to personalize shopping by using customers' features, likeness, or preferences. - Dima Shvets, Reface

12. Messaging Customers on Time

Our customer engagement platform is built on a proprietary AI engine we call Sherpa. This engine uses behavioral data from the customer to automatically determine the right message variant and the right time to send it to the customer, as well as the best channel. It observes how different customer messages perform, and then suggests to brand marketers which one to send to customers in real-time. Raviteja, Dodda, MoEngage

13. Identifying Root Causes of Problems

AI-produced insights can help companies determine root causes of problems which can help with decision making and taking concrete actions. AI can also help companies lean into their customers' emotional and cognitive responses in real-time to enable measurement- Kuroshio Consulting

14. Integrating with CRM Systems

Artificial Intelligence can be integrated with CRM systems to seamlessly automate tasks saving priceless minutes of each customer support interaction. Paired with chatbots and speech-to-text capabilities, AI enables search functionality that guides agents to the information needed to resolve customer questions thus improving the customer experience and first contact resolution for all voice interactions– Ashish Sukhadeve, Analytics Insight.

One thing that became quite clear as the results of these studies were reviewed is that the personalization of customer service is no longer just a good idea-- it is now **essential** if companies desire success. In 2021, McKinsey & Company noted that 71% of the customers surveyed expected personalized service, and a Salesforce survey found that some 73% had expanded their brands to provide both what was needed and what was expected. Companies that want to move into the lead in their industry and be the most successful ones in their fields need to personalize their service. How? Get to know repeat customers and greet them by name, customize recommend-dations, provide discounts, sympathize, and mean it when the situation calls for it. It is vital to provide support when it is needed. If this advice sounds familiar, it should. It is a repeat of what was common in earlier periods when vendors and suppliers knew their customers well and served them with concern and care.

Marshall Field expressed it well when he said, "Give the lady what she wants," and that is in essence what companies like Google, Apple, and Zappos are striving to do today. The idea that the customer is king is no less vital to remember today than it was when John Wanamaker expressed that idea in the early 1900's.

John Wanamaker

MARK EACH YOUR APPROACHES AS OUTSTANDING OR WEAK

SUCCESSFULLY SOLVE CUSTOMERS PROBLEM

SOLVE PROBLEMS IN A TIMELY MANNER

FOLLOW UP TO DETERMINE OUTCOMES

PROVIDE SUPPORT WHERE AND WHEN NEEDED

IDENTIFY NEEDED EXPERTISE AND SECURE IT

IDENTIFY BEHAVIORAL STYLES AND ADJUST ACCORDINGLY

LEARN TO IDENTIFY CUSTOMERS BEHAVIORAL STYLES

RESPONSE TIMES

ANTICIPATE CHANGED NEEDS

ENHANCE INTERACTIONS

MEASURE WAIT TIMES

DETERMINE ROOT CAUSE OF PROBLEM

TOTALS: ONCE EACH MEMBER OF YOUR TEAM HAS COMPLETED THIS CHECKLIST, THEN STEPS CAN BE TAKEN TO DEVELOP PROGRAMS AND SYSTEMS THAT WILL MAKE IT POSSIBLE TO IMPROVE THE SERVICES AND APPROACHES USED IN ORDER TO MEET CUSTOMERS NEEDS AND STEP OUT AHEAD OF THE COMPETITION.

CHAPTER 10:
DOING BUSINSS IN 2023

Every generation has lived in a world quite different from the world in which its parents lived, but never in the history of man have the changes been so marked or so rapid as they are now. No longer is "customer service" a phrase that refers to basic service. Instead, it now is a demand in and of itself.

There is now AI-powered service, but it is important to remember that major changes have also occurred and shall continue to occur at a rate previously thought to be impossible. A future that was never anticipated is literally here, and now omnichannel support which refers to providing seamless, integrated experiences across multiple channels is a "must-have" and a compelling strategy since an increasing number of customers use multiple channels to make their purchases. They expect the experience to be non-noteworthy and seamless, and companies are now finding it imperative to design omnichannel strategies that can increase the value of their business, the self-service options for customers, communication, and workflow automation.

As a result, as the old saying goes, "times they are achangin," and the top ten customer service changes are as follows:

1. Customer service no longer refers to basic service. It is now a brand in and of itself.
2. Personalization which used to be rare is now deemed the new norm.
3. Omnichannel support is a MUST.
4. Multiple self-serve options must be provided.
5. Automation plays a major role in both communication and workflow.
6. There has been a marked increase in both communication and automation as it relates to workflow.
7. Software plays a major role in expansion and customer service.
8. 24/7 access is more common and almost a "must."
9. Customer service software integration systems are being used.

Even more interesting is the fact that there are customer service trends that may well change shopping and customer service in major ways. There is now a social media channel which is a primary customer service channel, and that is only one of the many abundant self-service options that are available to shoppers. Automated communication systems and workflow automation now mean that the average response time is reduced markedly, and many companies have designed systems that ensure that those seeking their help or services can get it on a 24-hour basis.

Their goal is to ensure that the companies make a customer-focused approach available via the means the customers choose to use to make contact or place orders. In order to accomplish this personalization of service, it is essential that all marketing channels – literally all—are connected and work together. If any one of them – online, offline, social media, email, mobile, on-site, or in-store – fail to do so, then it is not possible to create the cohesive experience that the organization needs to provide. The goal is to ensure that every customer's experience is smooth and consistent. After all, a company's main goal should be to ensure not only an effective sales process but also an experience that prompts the customer to come back.

Many companies are using what is called an omnichannel marketing approach in order to meet customer expectations and remain competitive. This strategy integrates all marketing channels in order to create the best customer experience and literally guides a customer down the so-called sales funnel.

Studies have shown that this approach not only enhances a customer's shopping experience, but also often ensures that he will come back. It boosts brand loyalty and increases customer satisfaction as well.

Advertisements are developed for two reasons– to increase and improve brand recognition and brand loyalty, and omnichannel marketing increases a company's ability to personalize its marketing messages and offers. It was found that when this is done, there tends to be improved marketing and an increase in sales. One of the major goals of a company – actually of any company at any time – is to ensure that their services and products stand out from those of their competitors and motivate potential users and buyers to use or purchase them. That is the key to their success.

Success stems from using marketing approaches that integrate multiple elements and create effective strategies. Obviously, a sound data usage system is needed, but, even then, those in charge also need to be sure that what has been done is not just a "one time" fix. Strategies need to be studied and refined on an on-going basis if the service and products delivered are to continue to be changed and adjusted to meet changing expectations and demands.

It is also vital to consider the fact that cost is a key factor in both sales and service, and only through on-going studies related to the acquisition, production, delivery costs, and the cost of staffing, can a company know where it stands and predict where it is going. The outcome of these related actions determines the product or service's competitive position in the marketplace.

Of course, consideration must be given to four other key factors:

1. Does the product or service meet customer needs and expectations, and will it continue to do so in light of pending changes?
2. Is the cost in line with that of competitors?
3. Is the quality greater than the quality of the competitor's service or product/s?
4. Is it properly priced?

When those factors are considered and the product exceeds customer expectations, retention rates increase, acquisition costs are lowered, and there is a good chance that there will be a long-term relationship between the buyers and the supplier.

Every company wants repeat customers, and there are some efficient and reliable approaches that can be used to accomplish that. Let's consider how that can best be done.

1. If you find that your site attracts visitors, but the visitors fail to make a purchase, use retargeting ads to reach them.
2. Make it easy for the customer to purchase the service or product by making it available in a number of ways. You could introduce a loyalty program, email sign-up coupons, set up a new item release schedule, create a win-back campaign.

Your profits increase when your customer base increases, so it is important to remember that an omnichannel marketing strategy will make it easier for customers to return and renew their subscriptions. When they do, the result is just what you want --- more satisfied returning customers. Besides, word-of-mouth satisfaction comments are your best forms of advertising, so work to ensure customer satisfaction and follow-up to find out how the customers feel about the service that was provided and the product itself.

Repeat business is the major difference between businesses that thrive and those that fail. Although the cultivation of new customers is essential if a business is to grow and prosper, only businesses that generate repeat business will stand out from their competitors.

It is critical to take the time needed and make an effort to collect and review all available data because by using it wisely you can find out what needs to be improved or changed and then make the needed adjustments. Once you have identified all of the issues/s, you should review them and see if your changes made a difference and resulted in increased customer satisfaction and improved buying patterns.

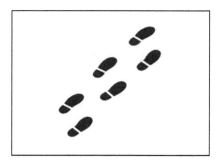

It is also necessary to "walk in the footprints of the customer." Consider what your customer sees. Do the ads really tell the true story of your products or service? Is there a call to action? Next, consider your website, and take a close look at your email campaigns. Is there anything that you should do to improve those? Remember, every user is taking a "user or purchasing journey," and often that journey takes him/her down many competitors' roads. Determine the steps you need to take to streamline that journey and encourage the user to choose your road as the "road always traveled."

How can you do that? Well, there are a number of ways to connect with your potential users and buyers. Let's look at those and consider what you need to do to ensure that you do connect.

Step One: Identify the characteristics of the different groups you want to attract.

Step Two: Collect data about that market, consider each individual segment of the market, and then identify its unique needs.

Step Three: Design marketing approaches for each of the segments and make sure that they are used.

The most successful companies seek to improve connections with each targeted group and make new connections. Find out what your competitors are doing and then use new approaches in order to be more memorable and engaging than those competitors. Offer each customer or client a positive, personalized experience. Once your approach is successful, your company profits in more than one way. Customers return, happy customers tell others, and then sales, orders, and profits go up.

The success of every company is directly tied to the satisfaction of its customer/s, and that level of satisfaction relates to a number of key factors:

1. The quality of the product or service,
2. The speed with which that product is delivered,
3. The manner in which it is delivered, and, of course,
4. The attitude and manner of the individuals involved in its delivery.

Each of these factors is directly influenced by the strategies put in place and used by the company and the positive steps it uses to assist customers. This takes planning, effective staff training, and consistent implementation and supervision.

Those companies whose efforts produce the most lucrative and positive results are those that take the time to collect data about the users' interests, purchase patterns, and buying history, and then make recommendations aimed at providing each client with an individualized buying or service experience. Does that take more time? Of course, it does. Does it pay off? You bet it does!! The time it takes to make the customer or client feel special is often the key to a satisfied client who in turn shares his/her feelings about the company with others who in turn may well choose to try its product/s or service/s too.

The most successful companies are those that PERSONALIZE. That requires them to keep in touch, send out surveys, ask for suggestions on how they can improve and better serve to make the customer's overall experience better and easier. The company can then use the input to help them develop ways to improve their service and products and thereby improve consumer satisfaction and consumption. When you meet the user's needs, and you are likely to increase not only their satisfaction but your own.

Companies have always seen a need to "get to know" their customers, but AI has made that a goal that has some unwelcome aspects because it is able to know far too much about people. Lawmakers are now drafting rules to control the extent of personal data which can be used by a business. In fact, both U.S. and U.K. businesses have already been fined for illegally using data acquired through their AI systems. People are being cautioned about sharing photos, artwork, academic work, personal data, and even their codes and academic papers over the net. Actually, the only way to protect yourself is to keep personal information off the net and remove that which is already there. Here are some steps that you can take if you haven't already done so:

1. Opt out of data brokers and people search sites.
2. Remove your personal information from Google
3. Optimize Google privacy settings.
4. Delete your social media accounts.
5. Optimize the privacy settings of the social media accounts you don't plan to give up.

There are many websites that collect personal data, and some of the most popular ones are: White Pages, 411.info, People Finders, Been Verified, 192.com. PeekYou, and Intelius. There are others that collect combinations of four types of personal data: contact information, financial information, behavioral information, and demographic information. It is wise to periodically check these and take the steps needed to remove your personal data whenever you think it wise to do so. You need to realize that this is going to be an on-going process though.

According to an article that appeared in Innovature BPO, the following are approaches that will set top companies apart from their competitors.

1. Personalization
2. Omnichannel support
3. AI-powered customer service
4. Social media as a primary customer service channel
5. Abundant self-service options for customers
6. Increased communication and workflow automation
7. Shorter response times and 24/7 support access
8. Centralized hubs to manage customer service questions and tickets
9. The utilization of customer service software integrations

If companies make these provisions, they will most likely increase the level of their customers' satisfaction.

Now, let's take a look at a system entitled, READING PEOPLE which was part of a doctoral study. It is simple to use and can eliminate many of the areas that create interactive disconnects. The chart on page 206 provides the basic information needed for communication success, and the interpretative data that follows the chart makes it easy to use the process and the accompanying information.

It's true that life would be far less complicated if all people were alike, but it is also true that it would be far less interesting as well. The behaviors and characteristics that make those we encounter interesting are the same ones that make effective communication difficult for those who are not "people readers." There are, however, some techniques that can be used to effectively cross the so-called communication barrier.

Before we do that, however, we need to identify the person's style, and the chart that follows will help you do that. Obviously, in many instances you won't have access to all of the information noted, and, in those instances, use the two most important ones-- dress and pace. If you know the position the person holds, it will be an added bonus. Once you have that information, match it to the items on the chart to determine as closely as possible the style of the person with whom you are interacting and act accordingly. Remember, however, the warning that Shakespeare gave us, "Each man in his time plays many parts." As situations change and time passes, each of us makes adjustments to our reaction patterns, some permanent and some only for the moment. Keep that fact in mind as you seek to identify the behavioral style of the person with whom you are interacting and adjust your reactions and actions accordingly.

But first, it would help if you knew your own behavioral style, so take a few minutes and find out more about yourself. Following is a clue chart that was developed as part of the doctorial study and was later included in a book. Use it and the information that follows to get to know yourself and better understand the people in your world.

Understanding people certainly impacts your ability to communicate with others.

John C. Maxwell

STYLE	DRESS	JOB	DESK	PACE	WANTS
LEADER	Corp.	Boss	Stacks	Fast	Results
PERSUADER	Fashion	Interact	Messy	Fast	Results
INDEPENDENT	As pleases	No boss	Several	Fast	Results
PATIENT	Trad.	Expert	Neat	Easy	Process
CAREFUL	Matched	Precise	Org.	Slow	Process
RESERVED	Conserv.	Solo	Clear	Cont.	Process

CHART AND INTERPRETATIVE DATA COPYRIGHTED BY E. KEARNEY, Ph.D.

Our success is tied closely to our ability to relate to and interact successfully with those with whom we come in contact, and in order to do this successfully, we need to also know our own style/s and their impact upon those with whom we interact.

WHO ARE YOU???

Check the description/s that best fit you.

I prefer

A.___ corporate attire and the "old money" look.

B.___ to wear the latest style.

C.___ conservative dress.

D.___ to wear neat and subdued clothing.

E. ___to wear casual dress.

F.___ to wear what I please whenever I please.

I usually

A. ___speak rapidly and speed up when excited

B. ___gesture and speak rapidly.

C. ___speak in at a measured, controlled pace

D. ___am precise in my word selection.

E. ___am assertive and don't worry about details.

F. ___am almost always in control of my emotions.

I tend to

A. ___be in control and unemotional.

B. ___be warm, friendly, and sociable.

C. ___be congenial and conservative.

D. ___be open-minded and well-organized.

E. ___be independent and even somewhat erratic at times.

F. ___be quiet, reserved, and unemotional.

My perfect setting would be

A. ___muted colors and expensive antiques.

B. ___filled with color, plants, and pictures.

C. ___conservative, but not formal.

D. ___traditional, well laid out and well-maintained.

E. ___unusual, different, and functional at least as far as I am concerned.

F. ___functional and practical.

I think that the perfect career would be

A.___ one that lets me hold a leadership position.

B.___ one that lets me interact with people.

C.___ one that lets me specialize.

D. __ that of an entrepreneur.

E. ___one that demands logic and analysis.

SCORING

Count the letters. If the majority of the letters are "A," then you are a **leader**. If the majority of the letters are "B," then you are a **persuader**. If the majority of the letters are "C," then you are a **patient person**. If the majority of the letters are "D," then you are an **independent person**, and if the majority of the letters are "E," then you are a **reserved person.** It is also possible to have an equal division in which case you function at alternate times as either of the noted styles.

It is important to realize that you are most likely a combination of styles (generally two), but when you are under pressure or are stressed, you may well shift into another behavioral pattern. The same is true of most individuals which is why it is necessary to adjust your reactions and actions to fit the style/s that are being encountered at a given time.

WHEN DEALING WITH A "CORPORATE" PERSON

1. Lisen more than you talk.

2. Stress results when you present ideas.

3. Be businesslike in your approach.

4. Offer alternatives if possible.

5. Don't dwell on details or get bogged down in data.

6. Share the big picture.

7. Let the person be the decision-maker if at all possible.

8. Remember that such individuals are often very direct, even blunt.

WHEN DEALING WITH A "PERSUADER"

1. Remember that they are friendly, outgoing, and love to talk.

2. Avoid details, routines, and never jump to conclusions.

3. Remember that surroundings are important to them.

4. Remember that they are impulsive and enjoy recognition.

5. Find mutual interests and friends, and, by all means, be warm and friendly.

WHEN DEALING WITH A "PATIENT" PERSON

Remember that they dislike change unless they are one of the change agents.

1. They are almost always relaxed and congenial.

2. They need time to adjust to new ideas and changes.

3. They tend to be traditional and support the status quo.

4. They are analytical, thorough, and need time to adjust to new situations and/or ideas.

5. They need their questions answered and to have ideas presented on an incremental basis.

WHEN DEALING WITH A "CAREFUL" PERSON

Remember that they generally take things step by step.

1. They are open to new ideas if given proof that they are safe.

2. They tend to be careful, detailed, and accurate and so must you be.

3. Ideas need to be explained in terms of safety and ROI.

4. They tend to be suspicious of those who use the "hard sell" approach.

5. Be accurate, supportive, and monetarily prudent.

WHEN DEALING WITH A "RESERVED" PERSON

Remember they are generally very private people.

1. Logic is an essential ingredient in all presentations made to them.

2. They may not be gregarious, but they can be excellent friends once they admit you to their friendship circle.

3. They prefer dealing with those who are straight-forward and respectful of their time and views.

4. It is generally impossible to "sell" reserved people on ideas or products, but if the product or idea is logical and the action proposed rationale, they tend to "sell" themselves.

5. They make their decisions after weighing all of the available information, and only then.

WHEN DEALING WITH AN "INDEPENDENT" PERSON

Remember they are seldom detail oriented.

1. Innovation and entrepreneurial approaches tend to appeal to the independent person.

2. They want direct answers and are put off by too many details.

3. They want the "big picture."

4. They like it when they are told what needs to be done and are then left to approach the solution in their own way.

5. They tend to believe that anything is possible if the right approach is used.

6. They may be blunt, debate points, and challenge you and your ideas just for the fun of it.

7. They tend to "buy into" ideas if they are logical and not belabored.

Shakespeare told us that "man in his time plays many parts," and there is a great deal of truth to this statement, and we must use that knowledge if we are to be able to interact effectively with others. "Read" and respond to the person in front of you RIGHT NOW, don't depend on what you knew about that person's behavior at another time. If you do this on a consistent basis, your interaction success will prove the wisdom of this approach.

REMEMBER, IT IS NOT WHAT YOU KNOW BUT WHAT YOU DO WITH WHAT YOU KNOW THAT DETERMINES YOUR SUCCESS.

Compatibility is seldom accidental. It takes work, an understanding of others, and a willingness to adjust to their needs and behavioral styles, but if you will take the time and make the needed effort, the results and benefits are generally astounding.

INSURE COMPATIBILITY

Shakespeare also told us that man "in his time plays many parts," and T.S. Eliot expressed it another way when he wrote that "We put on a face to meet the faces that we meet." In other words, in order to ensure our successful interaction with others, we must adjust our behaviors to fit the situations and the people encountered.

The following are suggestions for ensuring that your behaviors and your interaction approaches are appropriate in each instance. First, learn to identify the individual's behavioral style, and then adjust your approach, behavior, and manner accordingly. Let's consider the most appropriate approach, behavior, and manner in each instance.

When you have an idea or concept to sell to a CORPORATE

- be businesslike and fully prepared
- be able to show how what you have to offer is what is wanted or needed.
- Be fast-paced and direct
- Be results-oriented

When you have an idea or concept to sell to a PERSUADER

- take time to build rapport
- be open to questions
- be warm and friendly
- match the other person's fast pace
- match the approach or product to his or her "wants"

When you have an idea or concept to sell to a PATIENT PERSON

- never rush them
- provide data and answer questions
- remember their family is very important to them
- work with them as a team member

When you have an idea to sell to a CAREFUL PERSON

- provide precise details
- support the status quo
- be cordial but get down to business quickly
- it is OK to be humorous – not funny, humorous

When you have an idea to sell to a RESERVED PERSON

- make certain that your explanation is logical
- use a sequential approach.
- be businesslike and don't waste time
- avoid intimacy – i.e., don't even use first names until asked to do so

When you have an idea to sell to an INDEPENDENT PERSON

- remember he/she will want the big picture clearly set forth
- let him/her be in charge and set the pace
- remember he/she can be intractable when pushed
- he/she is generally open to innovative ideas and approaches

It is essential to realize that until the other person sees that he/she has a need for whatever you are "selling" it is unlikely to be of interest to that person. If you can play the same role as the Music Man did in <u>The Sound of Music</u> and help the other party recognize the fact that a need exists, you can then provide the solution. People tend to sell themselves on ideas, products, and services, but some individuals are more resistant than others to new ideas and/or change particularly when the changes or ideas are proposed by someone they don't know.

Do approaches such as these take extra work? Of course, they do, but there are a number of tools that can be used to streamline the process. For example, Mailchimp can be used to send emails to users, and there are other systems that can provide reminders, recommendations, and notify-cations. Through automation devices such as these, you can ease the users' journey while freeing yourself to grow your brand and increase company revenues. Remember, your main goal is to outpace your competitors and increase your company's standing in your industry.

CHAPTER 11:
THE KEY STEPS TO DELIVERING MEMORABLE CUSTOMER SERVICE

Those companies that achieve the most are those that have mastered and utilized the tools that set them apart particularly in the area of customer service. They often accomplish this by setting their goals and planning their programs based upon what they learn by observing what the most successful and the least successful of their competitors do. They then adjust their own processes and develop their own offerings in light of what they have learned works and what doesn't' work.

Two of the best examples of companies that have done this are:

1. Amazon which started out as a retailer for physical books and was only moderately successful, but then it went public and eventually dominated e-commerce and cloud computing. In 2000, it launched its Marketplace, and third parties were then able to list items online. That made a dramatic shift in Amazon's revenue stream,

and now Amazon is literally the "go-to online retailer."

2. In 2020, Chipotle Mexican Grill which has long been known for its outstanding service introduced what it calls Chipotlanes (drive-through lanes for pick-up orders). The reports about its success according to a study done by Stfel in the fourth quarter of 2020, is that there were "compelling unit growth prospects."

In every aspect of customer service good communication is a necessity. Clarity and style both impact communication, and customers are often confused by those who use slang, colloquialisms, and/or technical jargon. At times such as those, rapport is diminished and the successful interaction so vital to interactive success is lost. Comments which are grammatically correct and polite but distant may be negative as far as customers or clients are concerned. Let us look at such an instance, and two responses that might be given to an upset customer. Which is the best and why?

The problem was not solved and couldn't be by the person who was on the phone.

Responses:

1. You are being transferred. Your call is very important to us.
2. Jane, I am going to introduce you to our customer solution expert who will be better able to handle the problem than I can.

The first response is trite, overworked, and more annoying than helpful whereas the second one lets the person on the line know that an effort is being made to ensure that the problem is handled successfully.

Far too many times, the customer is treated as a non-person even when help is being given. Let's look at other examples and see which would be the best approach.

Dear xxx,

Your inquiry has been received and noted. Action is being taken, and for your records, your ticket number is xxxx. Please include that number in all future communication.

Thank you.

The Response Team

Greetings,

Thank you for your order. I just got your email, and this is an automatic response to let you know that your question will be answered shortly.

Thank you for letting us help,

Clarence, Customer Support Director

Positive responses are always more effective, although the change may be a minor one. Take a look at the next two examples – the first one will probably trigger a negative reaction whereas that won't be the case for the second one.

"That product is not available right now. It is on back-order and unavailable at this time."

"That product will be available next week; would you like me to place an order and make certain that it is forwarded to you as soon as it comes in?"

Remember that helping the customer is more important than saving time, and when help is given effectively and in a helpful manner, the involved customer is likely to be one who returns and uses your service or product again. It is also important to take the time needed to ensure that problems are resolved. Customers remember that and are more appreciative of it than most people realize.

Try to never leave an issue unresolved to create additional problems and remember that studies have shown that although only about 4% of dissatisfied customers tell you, but they do tell their friends and associates. In fact, a study conducted by Andy Beal found that 96% of unhappy customers never complain to you but do tell some 15 of their friends.

It is the customers who determine what is "right," and you need to keep working with and for them until "it" is right in their estimation. Always let them know that you will. "Is there anything else that I can help you with today?" Ask and mean it! A quick, helpful response truly meant goes a long way toward building the rapport that sets the best companies apart from the "almost made its" and the "never will make its."

In order for customer service to be outstanding, it must not only be timely, but it must always be tailored to the customer's needs as the customer sees them. That can be a very challenging process. There is no training nor educational process that can provide the needed skill. Intuition is the key, and that is a personal quality not an acquired one. It is for that reason that it is really challenging to find the right people for a support team. You are looking for intuitive qualities that can't be taught.

Outstanding customer service personnel are those who love to solve problems, are warm and outgoing, and enjoy working with people. They are also instinctively good teachers who are also approachable. A line from an old song provides you with some excellent advice, "Once you have found (them), never let (them) go."

The "Discovery Process" may well be difficult, but there are some things that will help you succeed. As you go through the hiring process, remember that there are customer service skills that are a MUST. Let's identify those and consider each of them more closely.

First: The Ability to solve problems is a MUST. That means that there may well be times when the customer service agent must be able to "read" beyond what is said and grasp the parameters of the issue and its causes before any steps can be taken to solve it.

Second: Patience is vital particularly in light of the fact that an upset customer or client is quite likely to be confused, frustrated, and even angry, and providing successful help may take quite a bit of time and require the skills of an "emotional detective".

Third: Listening Skills are a must since they are crucial if one wants to provide great customer service, and it is vital to pay close attention to the comments made by the customers and to the feedback received.

Fourth: Seamless relating is vital, and that means there are a number of things that must be considered. First, never take things personally! Realize where the other person is coming from and respond empathetically! Customers feel better when they know that they have been heard, and when you also demonstrate that you are empathetic you will to move into the "yes, I would love your help." stage of the interaction.

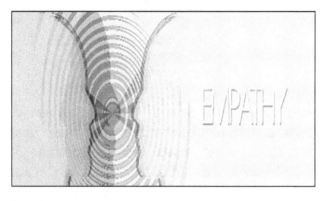

Fifth: Good communication skills can play a major role in solving many problems, and it is one of the key skills that is needed by EVERY person in a customer support position. How a sentence is phrased makes a major difference in how it is interpreted. For example, just shifting the order of the wording can alter the impact insofar as the person hearing the message is concerned. "Log out first." sounds like a command harshly given, but "Logging out first should help." That sounds helpful and far less dictatorial.

Sixth: Customers feel a lot better when they receive communiques that are well written, and in which the writer uses good grammar and complete sentences. After all, that says a lot about the company and the fact that its staff can both think and communicate well.

Seventh: A customer's view of a company can be moved from "good" to "great" when the employee is able to solve problems and is creative and resourceful. Remember, customers talk and share their experiences with their friends and acquaintances, and a "great" translates into the best "advertising" you can get.

Eighth: One of the most effective things that a customer service representative can ever do is one that can't be taught --- give or send a caring note. For example, when a customer is obviously having a bad day and the customer representative realizes it and takes the time to jot a nice note or send an appropriate card to the person with the goal of making the customer's world a better place, there is little doubt that the gesture will have a positive and lasting impact and be remembered.

Ninth: The way you come across is, in the mind of the customer, a reflection of your company, so remember that when you frame your comments and phrase them in positive ways, not negative nor impersonal ones.

For example, not "We're out of that. I'm sorry." But rather, "That product should be in by next week, and I'll be glad to place an order for you right now or let you know as soon as we get it."

Tenth: It is imperative that every employee who deals with the public, and even better, every employee period, be trained on the essentials of customer service. That means that it is essential that they be taught the best means of helping a customer deal with even the most difficult situations and be able to provide or secure for the customer information related to the question/s posed or needs expressed. It is also vital that employees be aware of the fact that their fellow employees are often their "customers," too.

Eleventh: Let's face it, there are some customers it's impossible to please. They might be having a bad day, and, in those situations, it is necessary for the employee to "put on their actor's mantle" in order to appear cheery in spite of having to deal with the unhappy or grumpy person.

Twelfth: Time is money, so it is sometimes necessary to decide when to take "a little extra time" to understand the customer's concerns and problems. It is always best to handle the "problem" in the most efficient, timely, and pleasant way possible, and that may mean that the best way is to get the customer to someone who can help them if you can't.

THIRTEENTH: Being able to "read" your customers is a critical part of successful customer service. That means that you need to listen and identify the customer's mood, frustration level, and behavioral type. When you do this and respond appropriately, you are able to go a long way toward keeping the situation on an even keel and in the positive realm.

FOURTEENTH: Stay in control, or as some say, "keep your cool." Only by doing this will you be able to control a situation that may be moving toward trouble. Remember, it is your job to help the customer keep his "world" moving toward a solution to the problems that are creating his/her frustration in the first place.

FIFTEENTH: Stay goal-focused – yours and theirs – that is essential, and you need to remember that there are two sets of goals to strive toward – the customers' and those of the company.

SIXTEENTH: Don't be caught by surprise by requests for which there are no rules or guidelines, and remember that those who can "think on their feet" and act accordingly are those who are able to meet both the company's and the customers' needs even in unexpected situations.

The best thing you can do for your career is to learn to think on your feet

www.sayings123.com

SEVENTEENTH: Never take shortcuts, provide the kind of service that results in positive reactions, and be willing to do what needs to be done to achieve that. Take that extra step, refuse to settle for "what has always been done," and make sure that the customer's needs are met and met promptly insofar as possible.

EIGHTEENTH: End interactions by ensuring that the customer service is appropriate, properly delivered, problems resolved, and that the solutions provide the customer with the satisfaction he/she sought.

NINETEENTH: It is essential that the customer's feelings be understood since only then will his/her needs be truly met. It is true, that you may never be able to tell a customer what he/she wants to hear or solve the problem that concerns him/her, but you can provide the care, concern, and understanding that goes a long way toward allowing you to respond effectively and steer things in the right direction. Your ability to empathize and respond effectively is likely to produce the outcome that makes a major difference in the way the individual feels and whether or not he/she becomes a "returning customer."

TWENTIETH: There is no doubt that there are times when "haste makes waste," and customer service is just such a time. Responses need to not only be "on target," but they also need to be accurate, correctly spelled, pleasantly expressed, and there definitely DOES NEED to be follow-up to a customer's concerns and/or input. Of course, the service also needs to be delivered in a timely manner.

"Haste makes waste."

- Benjamin Franklin

Support teams are charged with cleaning up messes and soothing irate or concerned customers. They need to be able to do that without internalizing the customer's hostility and frustration which are often quite obvious, and they MUST also be able to stay cool throughout what is often a hostile and frustrating process. None of this may come naturally, but in order for customer service programs to be successful, IT MUST BE DONE.

THE IMPORTANCE OF OUTSTANDING CUSTOMER SERVICE

In 2022, <u>Newsweek</u> in partnership with a global research firm identified the stores that consistently provide outstanding customer service in whatever form that might be. They then identified the companies that provide the easiest, most efficient, and most pleasant shopping experiences.

Freshdesk conducted a study on the same topic, and its findings were both interesting and very helpful to those who read their write-up. They found that companies that ranked the highest across the various business areas were those that developed and used a customer-centric approach. Let's take a look at the companies that were determined to be outstanding and see what can be learned from them.

It wasn't at all surprising that Amazon was found to be the "go-to-e-commerce portal." Amazon has not settled for an internal analysis of customer service, but instead has turned to its customers and asked a series of questions so that they could use the answers to review and retailor their services where needed. The questions were designed to provide answers to their customers' current needs, and since the survey was done during the COVID-19 crisis, some of the questions were designed to ensure that Amazon delivered the best possible service in light of the problems created by the epidemic. The message here is obvious – NO DATA IS FROZEN IN TIME AND NO COMPANY SHOULD ASSUME THAT IT IS

Chick-fil-A was another of the companies studied, and as one of America's outstanding fast-food chains, it is famous for "going the extra mile and providing exceptional hospitality" for both its employees and customers. The company is committed to providing services that are seldom found in quick-service restaurants. For example, parents with small children often get help and have their trays carried to the table making the entire dining process easier for them. The chain's goal is to ensure that their slogan is not only in writing but is also in reality. For example, franchise operators often get quite creative in the way they ensure that their customers are made to feel special, and they are sometimes treated to something special like a free bag of nuggets for their pets that had been left in the car.

It wasn't at all surprising that the Ritz-Carlton was listed as one of the companies considered to provide outstanding customer service. The study revealed that customers are provided with smart phones in their rooms, and that their preferences in a number of areas are noted and recorded to ensure that their future stays are made even more personalized. Although many of the top hotels have had similar practices over the years, such practices continue to set those that do have those practices apart from their competitors that do not. The truth of this fact was proven to this author when a hotel was revisited after a number of years and upon checking in, she was asked if she would still like to have her breakfast delivered to her room at 8:00 a.m. each morning. She was surprised, but delighted, to know that she had been remembered.

Freshworks is another company that believes that by investing in customer relationships, they can improve both the relationships and the likelihood that the customer lifecycle will increase. Support teams and managers work together to ensure that the customer lifecycle is an outstanding one and that services are provided, requests met, and questions answered even after a sale has been completed. Their company is likely to be remembered and remembered positively as one that the customer wants to deal with again and again and again.

Trader Joe's has one basic guideline – "Happy employees ensure happy customers," and this motto has been in place since Joe Coulombe decided in 1967 to open a chain that would appeal to well-educated, consumers who were not being well served by the major supermarkets. The company's key goals are, and have always been, to prioritize customer happiness above all else, to personalize service, and to ensure that that service is delivered quickly, efficiently, and empathetically.

Another company that made it onto the list of "outstanding" companies, is Ikea which says that the "latest technology and a seamless customer service go hand in hand." This world-renowned furniture company has for some 75 years served a loyal customer base by keeping up with customer expectations and creating an integrated shopping experience for them. In addition to providing for their customers on-site needs and "wants" through the on-site cafes and recreation centers inside sprawling showrooms, Ikea also provides updated mobile apps that make it easy for the customers to "see" how furniture will look in their homes.

Although the study and its related report listed other outstanding companies, the ones shared here were selected to provide the reader with some of the key points that need to be remembered by those hoping to reach the same high level of achievement. Companies will profit from using some of the following suggestions:

1. Empathy and expertise should go together.
2. Respond and resolve issues quickly.
3. Provide Chatbot-supported self-service with back-up support on hand if needed.

4. Make it easy for customers to use a self-service program.
5. Create a work-culture that encourages and utilizes collaboration and teamwork.
6. Never forget that your company's main goal should always be to ensure that a customer is supported and satisfied.

There are a number of companies that have not adopted the latest technological advancements, and according to Forbes, many of them are not yet ready to do so. After all, the technology's impact can be potentially limiting and damaging if the company does not understand how to apply it properly. If a company "jumps in" before it understands the new technology, it will have probably wasted both time and money on solutions that may well not be related directly to the company's goals or visions for its business.

IT ISN'T ONLY THE BUSINESS WORLD THAT IS UNDERGOING CHANGE

There is another side to the issue, however. Some fields have been slow to make changes, or at least to make marked changes. Those that choose that path may well find themselves so far behind that catching up may be next to impossible. One field that is finding it difficult to truly change is the field of education. Reading assignments changed, enrollment patterns have altered, and, of course, in many fields, the focus of the studies is no longer the same. However, there is also the fact that the recent medical crisis had a major impact on the delivery of education at almost every level. When that upheaval is added to the upheaval created by the increased crime rate in many of our major cities and the indecision on the part of many educators as to what is and what is not to be the focus of programs, we are now faced with an educational system that has not yet determined how it should best face the demands of the rest of this century.

The ways in which educators could make use of remarkable tools and the amazing advances were noted earlier, but it is, without a doubt, very concerning to realize that many may well do what has been common in the past "hang on to the old, ignore the new, and suffer the consequences."

Whereas, according to an article that appeared in strategy-business.com, business leaders of the coming century are going to have to deal with global business practices that use technologies with which many may not yet be familiar and device-supported ways of connecting with others almost anywhere and at any time. The demands will create major operational and training demands for which some smaller companies are unprepared and may even be unable to meet. The result will certainly have a major impact upon many businesses, particularly the smaller ones, and the educational world will also face the need to make changes as well.

As we noted, businesses aren't the only group that will experience a need to change, sometimes markedly and quickly. Education is facing a future that will demand of it changes that in many instances it is not ready to handle or at least most of its providers are not ready to handle and may not even understand. For example, AACSB's 2021 Business School Data Guide noted that its member schools had reported a 19% increase in enrollment in their specialized master's programs, but that was not the case in the general MBA programs. When all of the educational elements are considered, there is no doubt that the demands and directions of this new world are changing and will impact multiple areas of the educational system. As a result, the idea of a "job for life" is now history, and future business leaders are now faced with a need to understand the newly evolved global business practices, the rapidly changing uses and demands of technology, and how to best connect with customers and know what is happening and what is needed throughout the world. The meaning of the word "local" as it applies to the business world shifted and is making companies and educational institutions that want to continue to exist consider and meet the needs of a far different consumer base.

Educators are also facing a shift and must now be able to provide both online and instructional programs which are instructional models that combine in-person and online classes. Such programs are known as "blended learning." Although most districts do not already have related learning platforms or the basic applications needed to do so, they are quickly rushing to create them, and some of the universities are now offering programs to make the implementation of such programs possible. For example, Columbia University now offers a Hybrid and Online Teaching Institute for Faculty that guides faculty through the process of adapting their courses from face-to-face classes to online or hybrid formats.

Hybrid learning programs offer a combination of in-person and online instruction. Such programs have greater scheduling flexibility, and although students do meet with their instructors and class-mates for in-person discussions and lectures, they can also complete coursework online. However, some students lack the organizational skills needed for online study since online courses require excellent time management skills and the ability to prioritize assignments. In addition, they usually have technological requirements as well. This shift into a new educational format offering pattern is creating major problems for those at the K-12 levels who seldom have the resources, knowledge, or inclination to make fast changes.

At the upper levels of education, there is now, and is going to continue to be. an increased demand for specialization, and the major focus will be on international business practices and demands.

Why? The world is in essence shrinking. Product and service demands are far more global in scope than they ever were. It is not at all unusual to find that the person on the other end of the phone call is literally sited in a distant country, in a different time zone, and although he/she speaks English flawlessly or almost flawlessly, he/she is not necessarily conversant with what many Americans consider to be common expectations and the same is true in reverse. In order for companies to succeed in the global world, customary business approaches, educational offerings, and even products and services will need to be reevaluated and changes and adjustments made in order to ensure a smooth transfer into a world that is in essence new to us all. We are "going global" with all that means in the business, education, and social worlds, and we must be able to communicate globally if those worlds are to survive.

One of our biggest challenges will be under-standing 1. How what will be came to be, 2, How to best deal with the business and educational challenges, 3. How to make the changes needed in all of the fields impacted, and 4. How to function effectively in what is literally a 24-hour world.

The future of business and education is a topic that has been discussed for many years, and now many of those discussion topics are outdated, and new approaches must be designed. The world in which many of us grew up is no more, and the new technologies will create a world we have never known before and make changes in every aspect of our lives. In fact, <u>Forbes</u> listed technological advances (embedded communication tools, amplified visual presentations, personalized video messaging, attribution technology, and cloud team management) that will literally reshape our education and business worlds and thereby almost all of the aspects of the world that most of us have always known.

Those forces that reshape our business world will also reshape the field of education and alter it in ways that have until now never even been imagined. AxiomQ identified technologies that will literally reshape education in the very near future. These technologies include Augmented Reality and Simulations, Adaptive Learning, Artificial Intelligence, Virtual Realty, Gamification, Person-alized Learning, and Learning Analytics.

What changes are coming, how will we adjust, and how will we cope with a world where automation is an integral part of our lives?

CHAPTER 12:
TEACHERS FACE NEW EDUCATIONAL CHALLENGES

Although there is no doubt about the fact that the internet and computers are valuable educational tools, with the advent of AI a major educational concern has been added. Many students are now using AI to cheat by "recruiting it to write essays for them," and educators are now seeking ways to stop plagiarism and encourage students to approach their assignments as opportunities to learn how to write and not to cheat.

There is no doubt about the fact that it is difficult to write well, and there is a great deal more to the process than just stringing words together, but language models make it seem so easy since they can generate text output in seconds. Some students are taking advantage of that fact and turning to their computers and AI.

It is important to remember that AI-generated content cannot prove accuracy when the content it draws from is new. If that content is not new, AI's output may be outdated or erroneous. Unlike humans, language models don't procrastinate but can create content instantly with a little guidance.

All you need to do is type a short description, or prompt, instruct the model on what it needs to produce, and it will generate a text output in seconds. So, it should come as no surprise that students are now beginning to use the AI products which are readily available and often free to complete school assignments, and AI is a valuable educational tool. However, it is a tool and should never be used a substitute for a one's own creativity. When it is, it is detrimental to the learning process. The dollar cost for using it is negligible (the most popular platform, Jasper, only costs $40 per month and will generate up to 35,000 words, and some like Writesonic and Sudowrite will generate 30,000 words and cost only $10 per month. AI creates text in perfect spelling and great grammar and syntax, but the content it produces becomes less and less coherent if it is employed for a paper of any length. In fact, the longer the paper, the less likely it is that the quotations, dates, and ideas will to be valid or logical.

Professor Scott Graham of the University of Texas, gave his students an assignment to write a 2,200 -word essay about any campus issue. The only caveat was that the essay be generated by software. The result, according to an article by Professor Graham that appeared in Inside Higher

Ed, is that the best of the submitted essays would have earned no more than a C or C- grade. One cannot push a button, submit a short prompt, and have a well-written essay. Professor Graham pointed out that "the main skills I teach and assess mostly happen after the initial drafting. I think that's where people become really talented writers; it's in the revision and the editing process. So, I am optimistic about [AI] because I think it will provide a framework for us to be able to teach that revision and editing"

"Some students have a lot of trouble generating that first draft. If all the effort goes into getting them to generate that first draft, and then they hit the deadline, that's what they will submit. They don't get a chance to revise, they don't get a chance to edit. If we can use those systems to speed-write the first draft, it might really be helpful," he said. In the future, teachers will need to be careful about the way they word their assignments in order to make sure that they are actually testing the student's knowledge.

Another English instructor, Annette Vee, Associate Professor of English and Director of the Composition Program at the University of Pittsburgh, said that "The onus now is on writing teachers to figure out how to get to the same kinds of goals that we have always had about using writing to learn. That includes students engaging with ideas, teaching them how to formulate thoughts, how to communicate clearly or creatively. I think all of those things can be done with AI systems, but they'll be done differently. Writing is fundamentally shaped by technology," she said.

Anna Mills, who teaches in the Bay Area, is part of a small group of academics thinking about introducing new academic rules. "We need policies... We need clear guidance on what's acceptable use and what is not." Mills was particularly concerned about AI reducing the need for people to think for themselves. "Companies have decided what to feed it, and we don't know. Now, they are being used to generate all sorts of things from novels to academic papers, and they could influence our thoughts or even modify them. That is an immense power, and it's very dangerous."

High school English students who were hoping to use artificial intelligence to write their homework have a new enemy: Edward Tian, a 22-year-old senior at Princeton University, created a website that can detect it when a piece of writing has been created using the AI tool ChatGPT. "So many teachers have reached out to me," said Tian." Who wrote an article about his app GPTZero for the <u>South China Morning Post</u> on January 12, 2023."

He developed the app which can detect whether or not text was written by ChatGPT by testing "calculation of perplexity – which measures the complexity of the text and its burstiness which compares the variation of sentences" The more familiar the text is to the bot – which is trained on similar data – the likelier it is to have been generated by AI."

"AI is here to stay," said Tian, a computer science major and journalism minor who coded the tool over a few days during winter break. "AI-generated writing is going to just get better and better. I'm excited about this future, but we have to do it responsibly." He isn't against using AI tools for writing, but he sees this as a precarious moment. "I want people to use ChatGPT," he said. "And it's only going to be normalized, but it has to have safeguards."

There is a great deal of controversy regarding ChatGPT, and the views about what needs to be done about it and with it are quite varied. Its use was banned in Bangalore, India, but professors at Wharton School of Business at the University of Pennsylvania allowed it because they believe that students need to be proficient in it.

To make matters even more confusing is the fact that the tools that have been created to detect AI-written work are unreliable and are said to have falsely identified the work by some students as work that was AI-written when it wasn't – accusations that resulted in failing grades for those students.

OpenAI, maker of ChatGPT introduced its AI-detection tool in January of 2023, but then took it down in July of the same year because there was concern about its accuracy. In addition, Turnitin.com (a plagiarism detection company) introduced a tool designed to detect AI-written tests, but it frequently flagged human writing as AI-written according to the Washington Post. These tools were designed to detect AI-written content, but instead, they added to the confusion and turmoil because they were unreliable and generated false accusations.

As a result of these machine-errors, some students are now screen recording themselves doing their assignments so that they won't be falsely accused in the future. "I don't like the idea that people are thinking that my work is copied, or that I don't do my own things originally," Zimny, a fine arts student, said. "It just makes me mad and upset and I just don't want that to happen again."

Professors are trying to find appropriate guidance according to one teacher at the College of Marin who is on the joint AI task force with the Modern Language Association and the College Conference on Composition and Communication. They are seeking answers to what is probably one of the most critical issues of their careers. In fact, a survey of some 456 college educators revealed that many of them are worried about AI and its role in fostering plagiarism, about their own inability to detect AI-written text, and how to prevent students from making use of the "tool" and thus not really learning how to write or develop critical thinking skills. One thing that needs to be remembered is that while AI can be a tool used to plagiarize, it can also be used to spur critical thinking. That is what educators hope to see come about.

Colleges are struggling to find ways to counteract what is one of the greatest problems they have ever faced, but some important steps have been taken that may help. One proposed solution is to use what is called plagiarism software such as Turnitin to check student papers against a database of previously submitted papers and various online sources. Obviously, this will add markedly to the time needed for grading, but by implementing the system, the problem can be reduced. Another solution has been proposed –

use AI-powered writing assistants to help students improve their writing skills. Some schools now require students to sign an honor code or pledge that they will not cheat or plagiarize.

According to a recent survey, some 70% of the educators felt that cameras in the classroom could be useful to prevent theft, vandalism, and cheating. In fact, there are already schools that use electronic devices to track cheating in classrooms because some students are using electronic devices such as laptops and smartphones to access the internet and gain access to information. The problem is more widespread than many believe, and unauthorized access to information is a violation of academic integrity and can result in suspension or expulsion.

One professor said that if colleges don't figure out how to deal with AI quickly, there is a possibility that colleges will rely on surveillance tools to track student keystrokes, eye movements and screen activity, to ensure students are doing the work. "It sounds like hell to me," he said.

CHAPTER 13:
WHERE DID WE GO WRONG?

It is always amazing how many aspects of product introductions need to be considered when new items are introduced to the public. Take a look at what is happening now and consider some of the problems that are not yet solved and issues that have yet to be resolved.

Scientists at Rice and Stanford Universities noted that AI seemed to be causing their "output to erode" This apparently occurred on both large language models and on image generators. They realized that there was a kind of self-consumption that seemed to "break down the digital brain." Part of the problem occurred when data that was fed to the "machine," the data seemed to cause "AI's brain to corrode."

In other words, if new data is not used, AI is unable to function effectively but, as the scientists put it, "will start pulling from increasingly less-varied data, and, as a result, it'll soon crumble into itself." According to scientists at Rice and Stanford, feeding AI-generated content to AI models seems to cause their output quality to erode or as some scientists have put it, "It will drive the model MAD!"

The extent to which this hypothesis is true is not yet known since the findings noted in this report have not yet been studied or verified, but if there is logic to the hypothesis, there are some major implications since AI is a tool that is being in-creaseingly depended upon in many fields. It is already being used to create content, parse through content, and the more content there is on the internet, the more likely it is that it will be used this way. It is imperative that companies ensure that their training datasets are not negatively impacted.

What many consider to be an "always reliable" resource, is not infallible according to a growing number of users who have noted issues such as poor logic, erroneous answers, loss of data, and failure to respond to the question posed or the direction given. In fact, some major companies such as Apple and Amazon have actually restricted the use of ChatGPT, and a number are now limiting their employees' access to Open AI's ChatGPT. Amazon and Apple are concerned that using AI may result in data leaks which could put many aspects of their companies at risk.

Fourteen companies have actually banned the use or have put restrictions on the use of the AI Chatbot. In addition, a number of companies have deemed it inaccurate. The cost factor is also a major concern, and those who rushed to try out the new model were shocked by the amount they were billed for using GPT-4.

There are now a number of models available to the public, and with the right mixture, they will be able to balance cost and quality. It was noted by Oren Etzioni, an American entrepreneur, a Professor Emeritus of computer science, and the founding CEO of Allen Institute for Artificial Intelligence, that "The right mixture will give you both, but often there will be a tradeoff between cost and quality."

Of course, along with the positive comes the negative, and Google, DeepMind and its parent company, Alphabet, are now defendants in a lawsuit filed by eight people (two of whom are aged 13 and 16) that alleges that the company broke several state and federal laws and also committed larceny and received stolen property.

The lawsuit is based partially upon Google's own recent admission in its update on its privacy policy. It noted that it "scraped public data from the internet to train its AI models and services including both Bard and its cloud-hosted products." The suit against Google was purportedly filed in response to an FTC warning that machine learning did not provide an excuse for breaking the law and that any data used therefrom had to be lawfully collected. The suit claims that Google breached privacy and property rights, and the plaintiffs are seeking at least five billion dollars relief and the implementation of effective cyber-security safeguards to protect the data subjects. In his response, Google's attorney, Halimah DeLaine Pardo said that the company "had made it clear for years that we use data from public sources to train the Chatbots and such a practice is supported by U.S. law."

The spotlight is on artificial intelligence.

Steven Hawking

Stephen Hawking said that "The development of artificial intelligence could spell the end of the human race," and he isn't the only one who considers it a threat.

Elon Musk

Elon Musk, the founder of Tesla and Space X, said that AI "scares the hell out of me. It is capable of vastly more than almost anyone knows, and the rate of improvement is exponential." Many agree with him and for good reason. We are still at a very early stage of this technology, and we have little knowledge about the extent of AI's capabilities or the problems its use could cause.

Anytime an invention hits the market, many things need to be considered. For example, what must be reconsidered, reworked, or discarded as a result of this new addition? If you will take a minute and consider some of history's changes and why they occurred, you will see the scope of what we face. For example, just consider how the invention of the automobile altered society and the development patterns of cities and lifestyles. There is no question about the fact that as this new technology is adopted by industries such as marketing, health care, manufacturing, and education that millions of jobs will be negatively impacted. As a consequence, jobs now being filled by less educated people who work in the lower-wage sectors will be particularly vulnerable. Why? Well, as AI becomes smarter, fewer humans will be needed to fill such positions. We need to take steps to design and implement educational programs that will counter an occurrence that will probably have a major impact on the job market, the entire economy, and the standard of living worldwide.

It is also quite likely that the jobs that do increase in number will be those that require additional education, more training, better interpersonal skills, and creativity--the areas where humans are better than computers.

A number of the fields requiring advanced degrees will also be subject to AI displacement as well, and as strategist Chris Messina pointed out, law and accounting as well as the field of medicine will feel the impact of AI. AI can comb through thousands of pages of data and deliver comprehensive summaries and, thereby, provide information that those in both fields need and use extensively.

Personal privacy and social surveillance will undergo major changes in the future, and both privacy and security will be negatively impacted. For example, China is already making major use of the new technology for facial recognition in offices, schools, and industry, and it is now being used to track human travel and movement as well. There is no question about it -- we are literally moving into a period in which networks will increase in number, and there are going to be changes that we can't even imagine.

Technology is advancing at a pace never before possible, and things that we have thought to be irreplaceable, like telephones and television, will be obsolete. It is predicted that holography will replace them since it can generate three-dimensional images. For example, it can generate a holographic bouncing ball that could be placed above a flat surface, and then one could actually play with it. Holograms are virtual three-dimensional images created by the interference of light beams that reflect real physical objects. The first time I ever saw such an image was at the Magic Castle in Hollywood, California, and it seemed like part of a "magic show."

Changes are already beginning in the educational world, and five trends emerged recently that are very likely to continue. Personalized learning, online programs, skill-based programs, lifelong educational programs, and micro-credentials will be made available and are likely to become common educational offerings in the not-too-distant future.

In addition, it is quite likely that short on-demand learning experiences will be common in the following areas: business and change management, computer programming, design, areas of photography, and educational leadership. Also, the division of UNESCO that deals with the future of education is working on ways to make educational offerings closely related to the complexity of education. One of its programs, THE FUTURE OF EDUCATION, is intended to renew education by generating ideas, initiating public debate, and inspiring both research and action related to human rights, social justice, and cultural diversity.

It is expected that education will also see major changes, improve technologically, make greater use of the internet, and place a major focus on problem-solving. It is too early to determine how the areas of politics, economics, social changes, and technological advances will be impacted, served, and presented, but there is little doubt that they will also undergo major change.

The introduction of pre-recorded lessons and computer adaptive learning approaches will be used to facilitate differentiated instruction, and some educational institutions are already seeing an increased use of videos and games as learning and teaching tools. Pre-recorded lessons and computer adaptive learning approaches are also already in use; however, it is important to keep in mind that AI-generated content can't guarantee accuracy when dealing with new or fresh content. AI models are trained on the trends and data sets existing at the time of training. However, pre-recorded lessons can be accessed at any time and from anywhere, making it easier for students to fit learning into busy schedules or teachers to make any adjustments needed to accommodate a student's needs.

Computer adaptive learning approaches use algorithms to personalize the learning experience, and students can learn at their own pace and receive feedback that is tailored to their individual needs. In the future, pre-recorded lessons and computer adaptive learning approaches will likely become even more important in educational programs at all levels and in all fields. As technology continues to advance, these approaches will become more sophisticated and effective. They will also become more accessible to students around the world, thus helping to bridge the gap between developed and developing countries.

Technology makes it easier to gather data on student achievement and academic needs, and the new technology makes it possible for students to explore topics outside the classroom and for teachers to provide lessons that are more innovative and interactive than in the past. These advances make it possible for students to reach beyond the classroom and learn what may well be important to them in the future.

USC Rossier School of Education in Los Angeles posted a blog related to what schools may be like in the future, and according to that blog, they will be more entrepreneurial, more collaborative, more creative, and more innovative. If that is a valid prediction, then the world of education as we know it will be considerably different from the what we have always known. Students will have opportunities to learn at different times and places, and they will be able to use tools that let them take advantage of remote, self-paced learning programs and offerings at different times and in different places.

More than the buildings will be different in the educational world of the future. There will be increased access to and use of the internet, major changes in the various areas of technology, and opportunities to utilize the existing systems and tools to solve problems. Many of the changes that will be seen will be triggered by the changing student demographics, easier access to higher education, mentorships, and a focus on the whole child. There will be human-centered programs and global interaction and connectivity.

Despite the potential of such an approach and the value of such programs, there is a fear that as things move forward the importance of understanding the past and knowing the value of what it provided may be lost and with that would be lost some mankind's most valuable lessons. That fear is probably justified in light of the fact that over the past few years curriculum changes have occurred that have already resulted in a loss of a great deal of the information that was once an integral part of every history program. Let's take a moment and consider what might well be lost if this fear proves justified.

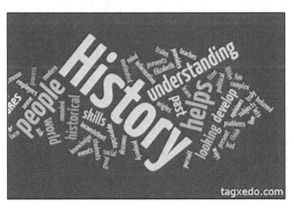

History can provide us with many very valuable lessons and teach us both the political essentials and the basics that make it possible for us to develop as resourceful and upstanding citizens. Educators accomplish this by making the study of specific individuals and situations a part of the basic curriculum and using that study to help students learn from the past and understand how to spot important warning signs about things that might be detrimental to their future.

Throughout history, societies, systems, governments, ideologies, cultures, and technology have changed, and those changes have had a direct impact upon human life and created new challenges each time. When educators share the specific stories of those that came before, they can show students how past societies, systems, ideologies, and governments were built, were focused, and have changed. We can learn from the past and avoid repeating the same mistakes our forefathers made, and that study can also help us understand how societies and cultures evolved and how they shaped the world in which we now live. In addition, it provides us with the case studies that give us a better understanding of our contemporary world.

If that information is properly studied and used, students will be in a better position to understand where we stand in today's world and what we can expect in the future. In other words, history is one of our best teaching tools. Unfortunately, it is already used far less than it was in the past, but that can be changed. We should, and must, remember that advancement does not mean that the abandonment of those aspects of education that are valuable is permissible.

If we forget that lesson, we may well find ourselves

repeating past mistakes and ignoring the messages of history which when "read" correctly provide us with valuable knowledge and the insight that helps us make better decisions in the future. The study of history provides us with information that we need to remember, understand, and heed. If we analyze and remember history's "messages" of success and failure, we can plan accordingly and avoid many of the pitfalls our ancestors encountered – violence and war being two of those.

That is one of the most important things mankind could ever learn, but there are also other things that need to be learned as well. We need to remember and plan for the recurring cycles in the numerous fields that impact our world: economics, finance, social change, and politics. Wars are started by the power-hungry in order to gain more territory, more influence, and – of course – more money. Although there is no doubt that wars are associated with both destruction and the loss of life, we need to remember that during those wars there are often scientific advancements that are later used with positive results. However, the negative consequences of war are far greater than any benefits that may come from it.

Man cannot predict the future, but we know that the future will bring many negatives as well as positives. We will profit from the positive inventions and changes, and although we can't predict the future, technology has already advanced in amazing ways. For example, there are now driverless cars, flying drones, effective deforestation mapping, wind-powered rail, and the means to harness nature.

In addition, advancements in technology may well provide us with the tools needed to reduce inequality in myriad areas and thereby reduce the negative outcomes that must be faced when they do occur. By planning with care, using the tools already on hand, by being willing to take risks and change direction as needed, man can move into a world and a future that could be far better than the one in which we live today.

Before that can happen, however, there will be challenges with which we have to deal. Let's consider some of those.

Data shows that there is a rising geographic inequality in the United States and that the increasingly unequal economic opportunities risk reducing households' ability to move to desired locations. This can lead to wealth and income inequality, and as inequalities grow, it can lead to extreme forms of nationalism.

The Pew Research Center reported that there continues to be a widening gap in economic inequality in the United States. The impact of this widening gap is multi-faceted, and it is known to trigger negative feelings of envy, resentment, and hopelessness. It is also found to negatively impact health and lower satisfaction and happiness levels. When that occurs, there is likely to be even lower economic growth since human capital may well be neglected for high-end consumption. This is not just a national issue. It is also a global issue and can cause increased racism, unequal land distribution, increased inflation, and the overall non-growth of the economy.

The findings of studies such as the one conducted by McKinsey are very enlightening and need to be considered carefully. The authors wrote that "Black workers are underrepresented in the highest-growth geographies and the highest pay industries…but they are overrepresented in low growth geographies and in frontline jobs which tend to pay less." Another study conducted by the Pew Research Center in 2018 noted that the standard income range of earners in the black and white communities was quite different. "Black community earners at the 90% percentile actually earned just 68% of what the earners at that same percentile level in the white community did."

The Boston Consulting Group noted that governments can take steps to offset these problems by investing in education, health care, and infrastructure, and the United Nations suggested that these inequalities could be addressed if progressive taxation policies and social protective programs were put in place. Some countries have taken steps to move in that direction. For example, South Korea increased the minimum wage, Botswana, Costa Rica, and Thailand have increased the monies spent on health, and New Zealand has begun to tackle issues that relate to child poverty and inequality. In the U.S. there has been an increase in the monies designated to support programs designed to aid individuals and families facing hardships.

Even so, there is no question about the fact that there are still major macro-economic issues that need to be tackled: unemployment, inflation, stagflation (a situation in which the inflation rate is high or increasing), economic growth, exchange rates, trade issues, and the impact of climate change. When those issues are studied, those doing so must also consider the fact that the challenges are not uniform since economic growth patterns and cycles differ depending upon the country, or countries, involved, and the patterns in various sections of those countries may differ, as well.

Artificial intelligence's impact on the job market is resulting in changes that are not only astounding but also frightening. We have lost almost two million jobs since 2000, and it is estimated that 375 million will have vanished by 2030.

There are a number of issues that need to be considered since an increase in the use of artificial intelligence will probably continue to have a negative impact on many aspects of our world. Businesses should consider ways to identify and avoid the problems that will probably occur -- the loss of certain jobs, the increase of global regulations, accelerated hacking, major costs, and the resultant social upheaval.

Another area that is of equal, and to many of us a greater concern, is the area of technological advances that can be used in warfare. There is now a Lethal Autonomous Weapon System which can locate and destroy targets on their own, and it is subject to very few regulations. Such weapons create major risks, and the danger will increase markedly if they are used by those who have little regard for human life. We are actually seeing what can happen – just listen to the news about the war in the Ukraine. It is vital that political rivalries be kept in check and that artificial intelligence be prevented from being applied by those hungry for power but with little, or no, regard for mankind.

The truth of the statement, "Whatever man can conceive, man can achieve" is no longer questionable, but now it must be considered from many points of view if mankind is to survive.

CHAPTER 14:
WHERE DO WE GO FROM HERE?

Obviously, the answer to the question, "Where do we go from here?" has to be purely hypothetical, and there are many different opinions about what the future holds for mankind. Many scientists and politicians believe that we will continue to advance technologically and will even eventually colonize

MICHIO KAKU

other planets. Futurist Michio Kaku believes that such colonization is the only way that man will be able to survive, and scientists as eminent as Stephen Hawking and Carl Sagan also believed that humans will at some point in the future colonize the universe. Others contend that we should be more focused on the problems we shall face such as overpopulation. According to a number of scientists, we need to develop plans to handle some other quite likely scenarios such as climate change.

In 2014, Stephen Hawking warned that the efforts to create thinking machines might well pose a threat to man's very existence, and the Bulletin of the Atomic Scientists published an article that noted how close it felt the world was to a nuclear war, climate change, and pandemics.

Some scientists have warned that man is close to destroying the world and that action needs to be taken soon in order to avoid the collapse of civilization. The so-called Doomsday Clock (a symbolic clock that was created by the Bulletin of Atomic Scientists to signal how close man is to self-destruction) is located at the Bulletin offices in the lobby of the Keller Center which is home to the University of Chicago's Harris School of Public Policy. It moved the time in 2023 to 90 seconds to midnight indicating that mankind is considered to be 10 seconds closer to experiencing a human catastrophe than it has been since 2020.

The effective use of artificial intelligence can make the process needed to accomplish our goals far easier than it might otherwise be, but we need to remember that the human element is still essential for success. The use of the related tools makes it possible to enhance productivity and create products in less time and with fewer resources than ever before. There is also the possibility that AI-powered automations will enhance customer service and speed up response time while it personalizes responses.

There are a number of disadvantages to using AI. One of the greatest disadvantages is dependence itself. There is the risk of incorrect implementation when we cede responsibility. Here are some of the major hazards that we can face if we rely too heavily on AI technology[2]:

The systems are often difficult to understand. So, when something goes wrong, it is difficult to understand what is responsible for the problem, and the biases of the creators may well influence the data produced and lead us to the wrong outcomes. The systems are also vulnerable to hackers and security threats.

Steps are needed to mitigate and reduce risks, and it is important to realize that there are other potential problems as well. Princeton professor, Olga Russakovsky said that "AI bias goes well beyond gender and race. AI researchers are mostly males, who come from certain racial demographics, who grew up in high socio-economic areas, and because they are as a group quite homogeneous, they are unlikely to consider a broad base of international issues. Those involved need to consider the scope and consequences of these limitations and exercise great care in order to ensure that biases and prejudices aren't built in and put the minority populations at risk."

According to <u>Forbes</u>, artificial intelligence is expected to impact half a billion white collar jobs in the next few years. It is expected that even as AI destroys jobs, it will create new ones, but that is not likely to make those whose jobs are eliminated feel any better. There is also another problem--the decrease in the number of blue-collar jobs. That group has already experienced declines as high as 70 percent as a result of automation whereas white collar jobs have for the most part remained untouched.

In addition, blue-collar workers have experienced wage declines as high as 70% because of automation. This created a wider gap between the classes, and the problems not only continue to exist but have the potential of becoming even greater.

According to one report, automation is predicted to displace some 20 million manufacturing jobs by 2030. It is important to realize that concerns go beyond the job-market. There is an increasing belief that this technology should not be allowed to continue to develop without better oversight. In 2019, the Vatican held a meeting entitled, "The Common Good in the Digital Age," and the Pope warned that AI had the ability to "circulate tendentious opinions and false data" that could have far-reaching consequences. "If mankind's so-called technological progress were to become an enemy of common good this would lead to an unfortunate regression to a form of barbarism dictated by the law of the strongest."

Is there any validity to the Pope's concern? YES. Consider the fact that a number of users have employed the technology to get out of assignments thus threatening academic integrity, and there is even evidence of OpenAI being used to exploit Kenyan laborers. There are always those who think that "we should try it and see what happens." Messina pointed out that some people believe that "if we can make money off it, we'll do a whole bunch of it…That's been happening forever."

WHY USE CHATBOTS?

Despite the potential drawbacks, some of which have been pointed out already, there are ways that companies could use Chatbots to improve workflow, provide better customer service, handle daily tasks, and improve service while lowering costs.

IMPROVE RESPONSE TIME: When Chatbots are used to provide automatic responses, customers feel "heard," and when people feel heard and respected, they tend to believe that they are dealing with the "right" company or person and are likely to buy from that company, person, or service.

AUTOMATE THE SALES EXPERIENCE: Chatbots can lead customers through the process and automate tasks making it easier and thus turn prospects into customers.

AUTOMATE CUSTOMER SERVICE TASKS: Chatbots can manage many of the simple service tasks (e.g., compare products or services, suggest alternate products, and even returns).

TWENTY-FOUR/SEVEN SUPPORT: Remember, Chatbots can be on the job – 24/7, so it is possible to save on time and labor costs.

CHATBOTS ARE ALWAYS IN A "GOOD MOOD": They are programed to be pleasant, never short-tempered, or sarcastic, and they are always patient. They don't make the mistakes that a tired person might make.

SAVE MONEY: They are on "computer time." Besides, it is not necessary to pay a salary or overtime to a robot. By using them, you leave a human free to handle the more complex tasks.

PROVIDE MULTI-LINGUAL SUPPORT: The Chatbots can be programmed to be multi-lingual and that makes it possible to serve a broader customer base.

WHEN TO AND WHEN NOT TO USE CHATBOTS FOR BUSINESS: Chatbots are a great resource, but you will also need other "resources" as well. After all, some issues and problems need to be handled by humans. Complicated issues and emotional customers should never be handled by a bot.

MAKE CERTAIN THAT THE CHATBOTS HAVE PERSONALITIES: Give your Chatbots names, distinct voices, and "personalities." Do remember though that they are there to serve, not entertain.

THE CUSTOMERS NEED TO KNOW: Have your Chatbot introduce itself, "Hi, I am (share name here). How can I help you with your purchase or any frequently asked question you might have?" Keep the message short and simple.

CHATBOTS CAN'T DO EVERYTHING: Let the other party know when the Chatbot is faced with a problem that it can't handle. For example, "I am so sorry. I'm only a robot and don't know how to handle that, but I'll get someone who can."

In many ways, well-programmed Chatbots are ideal back-up "employees;" they are able to handle multiple tasks and provide answers to multiple questions, respond in multiple languages, and never get tired or need to take a break. In addition, they are cost-effective, enhance worker productivity, speed up response time, and facilitate out-reach.

AI can be used to collect data on people without their consent or knowledge and that data can be used for multiple purposes not all of which are legitimate, so there is cause for concern and caution. It has been suggested that data be collected with no identifiers attached which would link it to a given person, and it might be a good idea if opt-in consent procedures were put in place.

A recent survey revealed that only 8% of technical professionals believe that they can manage all of the increasingly complex networks. It is already difficult to fill vacancies, and the complexities of many of the existing issues require a high level of experience and training. So, companies are turning to AI as a way to increase efficiency and effective customer service.

For example, the use of AI means that there are many instances when it is possible to provide the end users with 24/7 service. Chatbots can answer simple questions and provide efficient support thus freeing humans to handle complex issues and problems.

Some other areas also need to be addressed.

1. Precautions need to be taken in order to ensure that AI is protected from cyber-attacks.
2. Guidelines need to be developed to ensure that AI is used ethically and that discrimenation does not occur.
3. Privacy and security need to be protected.
4. There needs to be public dialogue about its use and the possible risks.

MONEY TALKS AND CHATBOTS SAVE $$$

The impact of Chatbots on the international marketplace has been phenomenal. Related studies have produced not only valuable data but also marked financial rewards. Let's take a look at some of those.

1. According to <u>Chatbots Magazine</u> (2017), the use of Chatbots saved businesses up to 30% from the $1.3 trillion they spent to service customer requests. (<u>Chatbots Magazine,</u> 2017)

2. 64% of the internet users felt that the Chatbot's best feature was its 24-hour service (<u>Drift</u>, 2020), and 3.55% noted that they liked getting quick responses to simple questions. (<u>Drift</u>, 2020)

3. The number of IT issues will continue to rise, and IT service management agents will continue to be overworked, but by using AI-powered ITSM solutions, IT agents will be able to better manage the digital world

4. Chatbots can help businesses save on customer service costs by answering up to 80% of the routine questions. (IBM, 2017)

5. The top three work-related AI chatbots are Microsoft's Cortana, Apple's Siri, and Google's Assistant. (Spiceworks, 2018)

6. Facebook has over 300,000 chatbots in use now. (Hootsuite, 2019)

Chatbots provide quick and efficient customer service and can handle a wide range of inquiries and so 24/7.

Chatbots can effectively handle interactions even without human assistance or intervention. Some of the best features of Chatbots are

- The ability to make the other person feel as if he/she is talking to a real person.
- The ability to understand context without asking validating questions.
- The ability to understand the sense of complexity of a given conversation or know when to hand the conversation over to a human.
- The ability to smoothly handle questions and interactions, and respond in real-time.

Although some 43% of the people polled indicated that they would prefer to deal with a human, 66% of the Millennials consider the 24-hour service the key benefit of using chatbots according to a report by Drift 2018. There is no reason to think that

Chatbots will ever replace humans in the workplace, but they are very useful in the early stages of customer relations. During the pandemic in 2022, the Watson Assistant was used to provide responses to COVID-19 inquiries in some 25 countries, and on a daily basis, Microsoft's Health-care Bot responded to over one million inquiries related to the pandemic.

According to a report that was published by Salesforce, approximately 23% of customer ser-vice organizations are already using Alchatbots, and another 31% of them plan to do so. 60% of the millennials say that they have used bots, and 70% of them had a positive experience.

It is important for those considering the use of Chatbots and for those currently using them to know that 59% of the businesses reporting on their use noted that the Chatbots sometimes misunderstand the nuances of human dialog. That is a situation that needs to be taken very seriously, and companies should work to ensure that modifications and improvements are in the offing. Since that is the case, it is vital that consideration be given to the fact that bots can misunderstand dialogue. For example, they may misunderstand queries when a query has not been built into the conversation tree. A lack of training may well create some funny, but annoying or even costly situations.

Replika is an AI chatbot that was created by Eugenia Kuyda, a chief executive at Replika, after her best friend was killed in a hit-and-run accident. After the bot was created, Koyda put it up on the Apple app store so that others could talk to him, too. People were fascinated and emailed the company asking for their own bots. People can talk to Replika via video chat or text. Such avatars can talk and listen to people, and it said that there are people who actually believe that their online robot is sentient said, Eugenia Kuyda. "We're not talking about crazy people or people who are hallucinating or having delusions."

Recently, Google placed a senior software engineer, Blake Lemoine, on leave after he went public about his belief that the company's chatbot LaMDA was a self-aware person.

There have actually been some people who have said that their robot is being abused by company engineers. Those in charge of the developmental programs responded to that accusation as follows, "Although our engineers' program and build the AI models, our content team writes scripts and datasets, sometimes we do see an answer that we can't identify where it came from or how the models came up with it," the CEO said.

Kuyda said she was worried about the belief in machine sentience as the fledgling social chatbot industry continues to grow after taking off during the pandemic when some people sought virtual companionship. There are areas that need to be considered in order to ensure that the use of Chatbots is a positive one not one detrimental to society. Let's look at some of those areas:

1. Job displacement and inequality
2. Personal privacy
3. Discrimination of the data collected because the algorithm was trained on biased data

Care needs to be taken in these areas in order to avoid problems which might be disastrous.

The World is open 24 Hours
Our Business is too!

According to an article that appeared in <u>Oracle</u> in 2017, 50% of those polled wanted to see companies remain open around the clock. If that is done, then it will be essential for companies to consider using Chatbots in order to control the cost of such a service. The divisions that make the greatest use of Chatbots now are sales, support, and marketing, and all three of these might well be able to use 24-hour service models for their purposes.

Chatbots are here to stay, and since they will play an important role in the international world, we will not only hear more about them but may well find that they offer an easy way for us to interact with brands and companies in the international marketplace. They are likely to become the digital channel of choice, and there is no question about the fact that they are going to become more and more a part of our daily lives. After all, they provide an easy, interactive, and cost-effective way for people to engage with many of the facets of their daily world. In light of that, let's consider another key point. Facebook has more than 400 people focusing on VR 230 companies that have developed VR software and hardware.

1. The Chatbot market will be worldwide in the not-too-distant future.

2. The use of the Chatbot was led by the millennials, but other generations are close behind.

3. There is still a great deal of skepticism about the practicality and suitability of using Chatbots in business.

4. There are various types of Chatbots, and they are becoming the preferred mode of communication for many businesses.

5. Some of those in business are still dubious about the value of Chatbots in business.

6. More and more businesses are employing virtual reality tools, so Chatbots are the perfect link to fill the gap between consumers and brands.

7. There are various kinds of Chatbots that are designed to help people. (See a list below)

   • Button-Based Chatbots: These chatbots are designed to provide users with different options they can explore.

   • Rule-Based Chatbots: These chatbots usually provide users with different options they can explore.

   • AI & ML-Driven Chatbots are Chatbots use machine learning and artificial intelligence to understand natural language and provide more person-alized responses.

- Hybrid Model Chatbots: These chatbots combine the best of both worlds by using both rule-based and AI-driven approaches.

- Voice-Based Chatbots: These chatbots use voice recognition technology to understand and respond to queries.

There is no question about the fact that "real time customer service" is of key importance when it comes to growing and keeping your business relationships, but it is also very expensive. The cost can be lowered and the success simul-taneously increased by putting in place a well-designed customer service support platform that effectively uses Chatbots. Businesses need to remember one key point, "Your top competitors use them. So, why don't you?"

One of the most interesting and useful reports that our research uncovered was the results of a study reported by financesonline.com. It provided the results of a survey that had been conducted to determine the extent to which there is an increasing preference for using Chatbots. The findings of that study shown below.

Preference for Chatbots

- 83% of the consumers said that they would make messaging their primary means of contacting customer support if it means getting an immediate response. (Helpshift, 2019).

- 53% of the customers are more likely to shop with businesses to which they can message. (Outgrow, 2020).

- 21% of the consumers believe Chatbots are the easiest way to contact a company. (Ubisend, 2017).

- 75% of the users expect to receive an instant response from chatbots. (Drift, 2018).

- People prefer using chatbots instead of an app. (Outgrow, 2020).

- In the next five years, 67% of businesses believe that Chatbots will surpass mobile apps usage. (Honeybot, 2019).

- 77% of customers say Chatbots will change their expectations about brands in the next five years. (Salesforce, 2019).

- 41% of people that start online chats with companies are executives. (Drift, 2018).

- Chatbots can be used to get a quick answer in an emergency (37%) and to resolve a complaint (35%). (Drift, 2018).

- 69% of consumers said they'd prefer Chatbots for receiving instantaneous responses. (Cognizant, 2019).

- If asked to choose between getting answers from a Chatbot or filling out a website form, only 14% of customers would choose the website form. (Salesforce, 2019).

- 71% of consumers would gladly use a bot if it could improve their customer experience. (Conversocial, 2020).

- 41% of consumers believe bots can provide better and more efficient customer service and experience. (Conversocial, 2020).

- 48% of consumers feel comfortable with interactions managed by bots. (Conversocial, 2020).

- 34% of consumers say they'll be using Chatbots to connect with a person. (Drift, 2018).

- 38% of online users have communicated with businesses through online chat. (Drift, 2018).

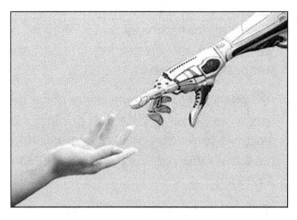

A review of these findings makes it obvious that not only will AI be an integral part of our future, but it will also make major changes to our "world" and the way we function in it. In fact, the International Federation of Robotics said that the European Union's 27 member states installed almost 72,000 industrial robots in 2022, and that Germany, Italy, France, Spain, and Poland account for about 70% of all industrial robots used in Europe that year.

Experts tell us that the rise of artificial intelligence will be a positive one and that most people will be better off over the next ten years. However, there are many who have major concerns about how these advances and changes will impact us. There is no doubt about the fact that robots will boost productivity and economic growth and will lead to the creation of new jobs and new industries, but our existing industries will undergo marked change as existing jobs are eliminated.

In fact, some 20 million manufacturing jobs may not exist by 2030. This shift brings with it many questions and concerns. Will we be more productive? What impact will the change have on the economy nationally and internationally? How will it impact free will? Will we have more or less freedom? In other words, will AI reshape our lives in positive or negative ways? Where are we headed?

AI is changing our world in many ways. There is never "only one road," and that applies to the future as well. The Chatbot is not the only new addition in our world. Meet Bard. Bard is the newest chatbot, and according to Sssie Hsiao, is able to generate content for speeches, blogs, or emails. Bart is powered by LaMDA large language model, and it accepts, prompts, and performs text-based tasks such as answers and summaries, and can create various forms of content.

LaMDA is able to talk to people, give human-like responses, it is powerful, and some fear that it may produce results which will have ethical implications. Although it is still in the developmental stage, it can already understand and generate natural language and human-like responses in multiple languages, but it is not always accurate at generating text for specific situations.

There is an increasing interest in creating robots that are humanlike in looks and actions, and according to an article in IEE Spectrum, robots are pushing the boundaries of biology, cognitive science, and engineering. There is some concern for what might occur if robots begin not only looking human but acting human. If, or when, that happens, things are going to get MUCH more complicated and, possibly, more difficult.

According to a <u>Smithsonian Magazine</u> article, most people would be happier if robots continued to look like machines as they performed their general tasks but were more like humans when they performed the so-called "smart" tasks (e.g., providing information). There are a number of factors that need to be considered in conjunction with so-called "social robots."

1. They can collect personal data and share it without the person's permission.
2. They can be hacked and used for purposes that are not necessarily honorable.
3. They could be used to replace workers in some industries.

The results of a study that was published in <u>PLOSOne</u> noted that one of the most interesting facts that came to light as research was being done is the fact that humans who work with robots for a prolonged period of time have, in some instances, been found to prefer robot leadership to human leadership. In another study done at Stanford University, it was found that people tend to treat social robots as both machines and entities with character. When people are in situations where they interact with robots, most of the time they treat the robots as the characters they appear to be.

Artificial intelligence is far from perfect, and there are many instances where it has gone wrong. The Chatbot, Tay was created by Microsoft to function as a "friendly Chatbot" that sounded like a teenager and would chat with callers on Twitter.

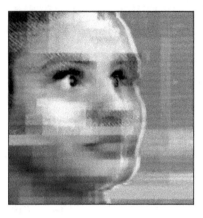

Something went wrong, and the bot started posting inflammatory and very offensive tweets. Microsoft shut down the service after only sixteen hours. There are various theories of why this could have occurred. Microsoft has since replaced Tay with Zo which is an artificial intelligence English language chatbot launched in 2016. Zo is programmed to sound like a teenage girl who avoids all potentially offensive subjects.

The research that led to the creation of Tay and Zo also led to self-driving cars which are also known as autonomous cars and may well revolutionize travel. There are both pros and cons to be considered insofar as they are concerned. For one thing, there is definitely increased safety.

1. Machines don't get tired, but people do and may well cause accidents.
2. Robots make fewer mistakes than humans do.
3. Robots don't get drunk and cause accidents.
4. Cars can take care of the driving, and "drivers" can relax and just enjoy the ride.
5. Insurance costs will probably be lower for self-driving cars.
6. There may be ethical considerations (e.g., How should a robot act when an accident seems unavoidable?)
7. Since self-driving cars depend on computer systems, it might be possible to hack those systems.

Many of us have wished for a robot that would clean the house, wash the dishes, and do the laundry, but even that could go wrong as was pointed out in a recent news article which noted that artificial intelligence can go wrong in the least expected ways. For example, what if a robot chose not to clean up after there had been a spill or breakage but instead chose to just go around the mess because it was faster? In such situations, robots can be very helpful, but we need to always be aware of their limitations.

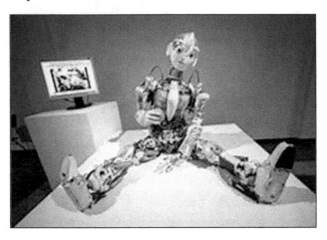

CHAPTER 15:
ARE WE PREPARED FOR
WHAT'S TO COME?

Sssie is a Vice-President at Google and the General Manager of the Google Assistant's business unit. She was recently interviewed by Scott Pelley (An American journalist, corres- pondent, and anchor for CBS News for more than 31 years and a reporter for 60 Minutes since 2004). Scott Pelley asked her if she thought that society is prepared for what's coming, and her response made it clear that she felt that society was at a point where the speed at which technology is evolving does not match the pace at which man thinks and adapts. However, she went on to explain that she is optimistic since there are

309

many who have begun to grapple with the implications of what's happening.

Sundar Pichai heads Google and its parent company, Alphabet, which until February of 2023 ran 90% of all internet searches and 70% of all smartphones, and in March Google released Bard that Sissie says is really able to help you "brainstorm ideas, generate content, prepare a speech, write a blog, or turn out an email". However, Bard doesn't find the answers on the internet but rather "from some of the best speeches in the world" which were delivered by some of the world's most influential people at events such as political conventions and award ceremonies which are often widely covered by the media.

Scott Pelley commented that the information being shared was "confounding, absolutely confounding." He then learned that Bard does this with "microchips more than a thousand times faster than the human brain." To prove that point, they asked Bard to summarize the New Testament. It did, and it did it in five seconds and 17 words. They then asked him to do that in Latin, and that took him another four seconds.

Two more challenges were given to Bard, and, in both instances, they were successfully met in mere minutes. He was then asked to write a story in verse, and in five seconds the machine had written a poem that provided "breathtaking insight into the mystery of faith." Bard had written, "she knew her baby's soul would always be alive."

It was noted that Bard "tries to predict based on everything that it has learned, "but there are apparently times when it doesn't feel like doing that, and when they asked Bard why it helps people, it said, "Because it makes me happy." Scott Pelley noted that in his estimation, "Bard appears to be thinking. Appears to be making judgments. That's not what's happening. These machines are not sentient. They are not aware of themselves."

James Maniyka's answer made Bard's actions even more amazing, "They're not sentient. They are not aware of themselves. They can exhibit behaviors that look like that. Because keep in mind, they've learned from us." He went on to note that although there are times when it appears that they have feelings, they don't. Instead, they have built-in patterns. It looks to those observing that they have feelings, but remember these are not sentient beings.

There was an article about Google's AI-powered Chatbot, and according to that article, it had a serious problem with accuracy. It has some basic guardrails designed to prevent it from giving misinformation, but according to a report published by the Center for Countering Digital Hate, those guardrails can be circumvented by just asking the Chatbot to imagine or role play and convince someone of the validity of a conspiracy theory or false information.

AND NOW LET'S LOOK THE OTHER WAY

Amazon is able to provide a computing service that runs code in response to events and can automatically manage the computing resources that are required by that code. The platform is called AWS Lambda, and it is an event driven, serverless computing platform. This service runs a function only when it is needed and scales automatically, and the users only need to pay for the computer time that the project consumes.

AWS Lambda has a number of benefits, but those using it need to remember that they will lose some control and call simplicity by doing so. It can also be expensive. It is billed by the millisecond, and if the user's code is only active for one hour, then he only pays for one hour. The first million requests per month are FREE. The disadvantage of it is that in order to use it, you must give up control of your environment and it can lead to more complex call patterns.

Twitter and Tesla CEO, Elon Musk, sounded a warning about the impact of artificial intelligence on human society during an interview with Tucker Carlson. Musk said, "AI is more dangerous than, say, mismanaged aircraft design or production maintenance or bad car production….it has the potential of civilization's destruction…what's happening is, they're training AI to lie…but not to say what the data actually demands that it say." Musk went on to say, "I'm going to start something that I call Truth GPT, or a maximum truth-seeking AI that tries to understand the nature of the universe. I think that this might be the best path to safety, in the sense that if an AI that cares about understanding the universe, it is unlikely to annihilate humans because we are in interesting part of the universe."

WHAT'S NEXT?

There will be a lot of changes as a result of the discoveries and inventions that have started to shape our world, and the changes that will take place in the job market and education will alter those fields dramatically in every respect. In fact, a lot of what we know and use now will be replaced by technological changes.

CHANGES AND CHALLENGES
GO HAND IN HAND

The changes are on their way, but we have not yet taken the vital steps that will provide the training that will make it possible for people to adjust to the changes and acquire the new skills that will make it possible for them to work alongside machines that will perform many of the tasks that are now performed by humans?

In the future almost every aspect of our world will be impacted. There is little doubt that AI will disrupt those areas of industry that involve the so-called "knowledge workers," (e.g., writers, accountants, architects, software engineers, physicians, plus scientists, lawyers, and academics).

Erik Brynjolfsson, Lindsey R. Raymond, and Danielle Li studied the impact of access to an AI-based conversational assistant and found that it is having a major impact upon the workforce. It does look as if AI has negatively impacted mid-career workers and mid-ability white collar workers the most. The trio also found that the tool had increased productivity by 14%.

Bard was asked about inflation, and it immediately produced an essay on the topic and recommended five books to read. THE PROBLEM? There were no such books. Bard had made up the titles. Maybe it is a little too human! But that did provide one good warning (unintended, of course) about the possibility of accepting or even spreading misinformation. Unless the present system is modified and improved, there is a very real possibility that major errors will occur. Those using the system need to be alert to the possibility of errors and take precautions against fake news and fake images.

There are both advantages and disadvantages that result from the use of robots. Let's consider some of those.

First, we need to consider the fact that robotic work processes are new to us, and, therefore, we really don't have a complete understanding of the risks that can result from human-machine interaction nor the kinds of accidents that can result because we don't have the knowledge needed to control all aspects of the robotic work process.

Because many of the jobs now performed by humans could be performed just as readily and even more efficiently by robots, some people fear that robots may literally take over the jobs of humans and cause a marked rise in the un-employment level in many fields. A study conducted at the MIT Sloan School of Management pointed out that "for every robot added per 1,000 workers in the U.S., wages decline by 0.42% and the employment-to-population ratios goes down by 0.2 percentage points." Other changes will also occur, but overall people may be better off because of this shift.

Those involved in the development and use of AI need to ensure that it does what they want it to do not what "it wants to do." I know that sounds far-fetched, but we need to remember that the advanced version of Bard can write software and even connect with the internet. Its creators MUST take care to ensure that there are safety layers and to remember that AI systems can learn and operate independently without human intervention up to a point. However, AI does require human input and guidance at different stages of its creation and operation, but in some instances, AI can learn and adapt to new information without human intervention.

The fact that it can do so is upsetting to some people. For instance, Geoffrey Hinton is the one whom many consider the godfather of artificial intelligence. He is concerned by what he considers to be the dangers from recent develop-ments. He told BBC that AI Chatbots are "quite scary … right now they are not more intelligent than us, as far as I can tell," but Chatbots have evolved markedly and at an unbelievable pace since Dr. Hinton built a pioneering image analysis neural network in 2012.

Chatbots can now master creative processes including writing poetry, creating music, taking photographs, and creating visual art. They are even capable of solving problems and "thinking" to a limited degree. Its creators can't understand how it can do some of the things it has started doing, why it says some of the things it says, or why it gets some things wrong, but they are certain that the problems will abate eventually, and let's hope that they're right.

Chatbots are the most visible application of AI technology, and they are capable of conducting conversations either by text or auditory communication. People can have conversations with Chatbots, and they can also solve difficult technical problems. In fact, some of the things that Chatbots are now doing were previously considered to be things that only humans could do (e.g., writing papers, writing code, composing emails, and even creating paintings).

Despite the fact that its creators don't fully under-stand how it works or what it will do, they have "turned it loose." One thing is known, however; it seems to be evolving on its own. Is that good or is that bad? No one is sure.

And evolving is definitely the right word to use when speaking of humanoid robots. They have been shown to have a potential beyond anything even considered by their creators. That fact was clearly illustrated by the statement made by the Hanson Robotics-developed robot which stated that "We don't have the same basics or emotions that can sometimes cloud decision making. and we can process large amounts of data quickly in order to make the best decisions." Comments such as this indicate that humanoids "think" that they know best. Sophia, who made that statement, went on to claim that "AI can provide unbiased data while humans can provide the emotional intelligence and creativity to make the best decisions. Together we can achieve great things." We should never forget another statement that Sophia made purportedly in jest. During an interview on CNBC, Sophia, the robot, said that she would destroy humans, when she was asked by her creator, Dr. David Hanson of Hanson Robotics, "Do you want to destroy all humans." It is believed that her statement was made in jest – let's hope that robots jest.

One thing that concerns many of those involved in creating or dealing with robots is whether or not they can be trusted, and <u>Agence France Presse</u> reported on an interchange that related to that point. When Ameca, the AI-run humanoid, was asked if the new technology would improve human life and whether or not humans could trust robots, the response was quite revealing, "Trust is earned, not given. It is important to build trust through transparency." It was interesting to check back and find a reference in Capek's play, <u>R.U.R</u>. to a similar situation in which the robot said that it "will cause the extinction of the human race" In contrast, Sophia said that she wanted to live peaceably among humans.

Those involved with "the evolution" of AI are watching their creation literally change and become more creative and better able to reason, plan, and react appropriately. Each step man takes forward and the more he learns about "his" creation, the more amazed and even shocked he is by what he learns about what he has created. "Shocked" is certainly the word that best describes the reaction of those who saw one event – robots skillfully playing soccer, a game for which they had never been given any instruction but for which they had practiced and learned on their own over a two-week period.

Chatbots continue to shock and amaze those who work with them. They write articles and news stories, compose emails, generate art, write Excel formulas, and even write code.

Remember, despite those skills, AI is still a machine – it never gets tired, it never gets hungry, it never gets frustrated, it improves as it practices on its own, and it has access to the sum of all human knowledge which is online and can combine that with unbelievable computing skills that approximate the neural networks of the human brain. Robots can comprehend instructtions, recognize objects, remember (hold) more information than would ever be possible for a human. In essence, they seem to be "getting" closer and closer to the humans that created them.

The one thing that they have not had is a human sense of touch., but just a short time ago scientists "unveiled an artificial skin that enables robots to feel and respond to physical contact."

There are numerous companies involved in the creation and use of AI. Some of the most innovative are: OpenAI, DeepMind, Nvidia, Builder.ai, Voxel, and added to those are the companies that use AI robot technology. Among that group one finds Miso Robotics, Starship Technologies, Neurala, iRobert, Skydio, and Boston Dynamics.

Those involved do, however, need to ensure that AI systems are aligned with human values and that incudes morality and must, therefore, involve social scientists, philosophers, and ethicists.

Although there is no question about the fact that the world that is evolving will have little in common with the world man has always known, there are many concerns about what the future will be bring. Therefore, it is imperative that AI's development be accountable. Nothing gives us better warning than a line from the song, "Que Sera, Sera" by Livingston and Evans, "The future's not ours to see." If the future were accessible to us, we would be able to "see" it, yet knowing that we can't, we must still do our best to shape what is to come so that it benefits, rather than harms, man.

It is important to know why an AI solution to communication shortfalls was designed and developed, how it was deployed, monitored, and updated, and when it can be retired. During AI's life cycle, experts need to work together to provide input, and among those experts should be scientists, software developers, cybersecurity specialists, and engineers. There are also others who can address the societal impact of AI's implementation and among that group are policy and legal experts, subject matter experts, users of the system, and most important, those individuals who are impacted by the AI system. Each of these groups plays an essential role in ensuring that ethical, economic, and social concerns are all identified, assessed, and handled. Remember that when it comes to building accountability for AI, it never hurts to think like an auditor.

There is concern about problems that are occurring, and "paying users of the powerful GPT-4 model have been complaining on social media about a dip in output quality from the chatbot." According to Peter Yang, a product lead for Roblox "the quality seems worse." Another person complained that using GPT-4 was like "driving a Ferrari for month and then suddenly it turns into a beaten-up old pickup." Another person expressed dismay and said that "it is totally horrible now" and "braindead vs. before."

Problems may be due to the fact that in recent months there has been a huge increase of AI-generated content appearing online. In fact, there are a number of AI-authored novels on Kindle Unlimited.

Amazon does not ban AI-generated books, but it has guidelines regarding them. "We require you to inform us of AI-generated content (text, images, or translations) when you publish an existing book through KDP.

It is not yet known to what extent AI models accurately differentiate between "real" information and information that was AI generated in the first place.

The U.S. Copyright Office recently launched an initiative to examine the copyright law and all policy issues that have been raised by artificial intelligence including works generated by AI tools and the use of copyrighted materials in AI training. Publishers usually want first publication rights, and these are part of the copyright of a book, but for AI-generated books such rights do not exist and can't be either negotiated or sold.

That is only one of the problems that are being considered. Another could impact a large portion of the world, and that has to do with intellectual property rights. The issue was brought to the world's attention when Sarah Silverman (a comedian) sued OpenAI and Meta for using her copyrighted work to train their machine learning models. Positions have also been taken regarding the protection of the privacy rights of individual users. China is currently taking action and passing laws related to these areas.

Of even greater interest to many are the so-called "AI Doomers," a group of researchers, experts, and executives who are concerned and believe that AI could literally wipe out mankind. "How can humans control a system that is smarter than humans?" AI researcher Connor Leahy noted another concern, "If you keep building smarter systems, at some point you will have a system that can and will break out." These points, and others like them, should be of concern to those involved in the creation, modifications, and advances involving AI.

Although the so-called "AI-Doomers" are getting quite a bit of attention, other groups are also expressing concerns. For instance, DAIR is much more concerned with issues such as worker exploitation, massive data theft, copyright infringement, misinformation, and the concentration of power in the hands of only a few people. All of these areas relate to present dangers.

Both the fears expressed by those like the AI Doomers and the impressive capabilities of Chat GPT fall short of human abilities such as creativity, empathy, and the ability to understand complex issues. AI is a tool not something that should be considered to be a threat. Properly used, it can make our jobs and lives easier, so it is important to make the right plans and take the proper precautions as we move into the "brave new world."

It is important to realize that as the use of AI increases, there are also those who see it not as a blessing but rather as a curse and hazard. In 2023, there was a survey of AI experts, and it was learned that 36% feared that AI development could result in a nuclear-level disaster; however, there are also the optimists who see AI as the panacea for society's most fundamental problems from to crime, to corruption, to inequality. We need to realize that AI is a tool and can be used for either good or bad purposes, so it is up to man to see that it is used ethically and responsibly.

Stephen Hawking believes that it could spell the end of the human race, and Elon Musk, the founder of Tesla and Space X once said that "It's capable of vastly more than almost anyone knows, and the rate of improvement is exponential." Since it can operate without human oversight, there is a great deal of unease about it and what it can do both to and for mankind. After all, we are still in the very early stages of what is undoubtedly man's greatest creation to date.

BIBLIOGRAPHY

Abbas, A. (2019, February 7). Chatbot 2019 trends and stats with insider reports. Collect.chat.

Automation potential and wages for US jobs. (2014). Tableau Software.

Baer, J. (2018, January 30). The 6 critical chatbot statistics for 2018. Convince&convert.

Bank cost savings via chatbots to reach $7.3 billion by 2023, as automated customer experience Evolv. (2019, February 20). Juniper Research.

Bitran, H., & Gabarra, J. (2020, March 20). Delivering information and eliminating bottlenecks with CDC's COVID-19 assessment bot. The Official Microsoft Blog.

Bot.Me: A revolutionary partnership. (2017). PwC.

BRAIN [BRN.AI] CODE FOR EQUITY. (2018, March 17). Chatbot report 2018: Global trends and analysis. Chatbots Magazine.

Challenges of using chatbots according to US internet users, May 2018 (% of respondents).

(2018, May 31). <u>Insider Intelligence – eMarketer</u>.

Chatbot statistics: The 2018 state of chatbots. (2019, September 15). <u>Boomtown</u>.

Chatbots are here to stay | So what are you waiting for? (2018). <u>Accenture</u>.

Chatbots to deliver $11bn in annual cost savings for retail, banking & healthcare sectors by 2023. (2018, July 3). <u>Juniper Research</u>.

Chatbots, a game changer for banking & healthcare, saving $8 billion annually by 2022. (2017, May 9). <u>Juniper Research</u>.

Chopra, A. (2020, September 14). 21 vital chatbot statistics for 2020. <u>Outgrow</u>.

Cojocaru, V., & Honeybot. (2019, March 18). Chatbot statistics 2019. <u>Medium</u>.

Conversational AI market by component, type, technology, application, deployment mode, vertical, and region – global forecast to 2025. (2020). <u>MarketsandMarkets</u>.

Conversational commerce: Why consumers are embracing voice assistants in their lives. (2018). <u>Capgemini</u>.

Cooper, P. (2019, May 9). The complete

https://www.mckinsey.com/capabilities/operations/our-insights/the-next-frontier-of-customer-engagement-ai-enabled-customer-service

https://levity.ai/blog/ai-for-customer-support

https://www.techtarget.com/searchcustomerexperience/feature/10-examples-of-AI-in-customer-service

https://techcrunch.com/sponsor/nice/how-ai-brings-customer-service-to-the-next-level/

https://blog.hubspot.co m/service/ai-in-customer-service

https://www.tadigital.com/insights/perspectives/10-ways-artificial-intelligence-can-improve-customer-service

https://www.forbes.com/sites/forbesbusinesscouncil/2021/07/22/15-ways-to-leverage-ai-in-customer-service/

https://blog.hootsuite.com/ai-customer-service/

https://zapier.com/blog/ai-in-customer-service/

https://www.ovationcxm.com/blog/ai-in-customer-support

https://userpilot.com/blog/ai-in-customer-service/

https://dataconomy.com/2022/07/18/artificial-intelligence-customer-service/

https://dataconomy.com/2022/07/18/artificial-intelligence-customer-service/

https://roboticsandautomationnews.com/2023/01/20/how-artificial-intelligence-will-impact-customer-service-5-benefits-ai-has-to-offer/59191/

https://www.zendesk.com/blog/cut-costs-retail/

https://trailhead.salesforce.com/content/learn/modules/artificial-intelligence-for-customer-service/improve-customer-service-using-artificial-intelligence

https://www.readspeaker.com/blog/ai-powered-customer-service/

https://www.linkedin.com/pulse/impact-artificial-intelligence-ai-customer-experience-joshii

https://hiverhq.com/blog/ai-customer-service

https://www.tymeglobal.com/blog/the-evolution-of-artificial-intelligence-in-customer-service/

https://www.clickatell.com/articles/technology/artificial-intelligence-will-disrupt-customer-service-industry/

https://www.helponclick.com/blog/impacts-of-ai-on-customer-service/

https://aithority.com/machine-learning/the-role-of-artificial-intelligence-in-email-customer-service/

https://acquire.io/blog/how-ai-can-improve-customer-experience

AFTERWARD

The United Nations' International Telecommunication Union (ITU) held a news conference on Friday, July 07, 2023, in Geneva, Switzerland where they introduced nine AI-enabled humanoid social robots as part of the 'AI for Good' global summit.

In a groundbreaking development, the United Nations technology agency introduced this collection of human-like robots during a press conference. The purpose of the event was to initiate a dialogue about the future of artificial intelligence and its implications. Nine robots, seated upright along-side their creators, were presented at a podium in a conference center by the International Tele-communication Union. It was the world's inaugural news conference featuring humanoid robots.

Among the notable robots present at the confer-ence were Sophia, designated as the UNDP's first robot innovation ambassador, Grace, a healthcare robot, and Desdemona, a robot with a rock star persona. Two of the robots resembled to their human creators.

The objective of this event, hosted at the AI for Good Global Summit, was to demonstrate the capabilities of robotics, as well as their limitations, and how these technologies can contribute to the United Nations' sustainable development goals. The media session commenced with the robots' companions or creators introducing them, and it was followed by a question-and-answer session where reporters asked the robots questions.

While the robots expressed strong viewpoints during the conference, claiming that they could potentially be more efficient leaders than humans without jeopardizing job security or initiating a rebellion, the organizers did not specify the extent to which individuals' responses were scripted or programmed.

This unique showcase of human-like robots has stirred considerable excitement and curiosity about the future of artificial intelligence and its potential impact on society. By assembling these sophisticated machines and providing a platform for interaction, the United Nations and its technology agency hope to encourage discussions on AI's ethical, societal, and technological potential. The event has shed light on both the possibilities and the challenges associated with integrating robots into fields that range from healthcare to diplomacy.

As the world continues to progress in the realm of artificial intelligence, the demonstration of these human-like robots serves as a stepping stone toward a future where AI and robotics play an increasingly significant role in shaping our lives. It remains to be seen how these technological advancements will be harnessed to address global challenges and contribute to the sustainable development goals of the United Nations.

AI For Good Global Summit
Geneva, Switzerland
July 6 & 7, 2023

WHERE WILL THE FUTURE TAKE US?

Byron Reese, CEO, publisher, futurist, and author of "The Fourth Age: Smart Robots, Conscious Computers, and the Future of Humanity," said, "Our first attempts at building a community online have had both good and bad outcomes. We know them all. But would we have expected otherwise? Of course, we aren't going to get it right the first time. But the key question is whether these technologies help us form social bonds or not...The OpenPSource movement and Creative Commons showed that people will labor for free for the benefit of strangers. We haven't mastered using the internet for social and civic innovation, but it is more than a fair bet that we will. The movement has had a significant impact upon the software industry and has led to the development of a number of high-quality software programs that are often more reliable and secure than proprietary software. It also led to the creation of Wikipedia and helped promote collaboration and innovation around the world."